CROCK·POT
· THE ORIGINAL SLOW COOKER ·

ALL★AMERICAN
MORE THAN 100 COMFORT FOODS ENJOYED NATIONWIDE

Publications International, Ltd.

TABLE OF CONTENTS

Creamy Farmhouse Chicken
and Garden Soup p. 74

SLOW COOKER TIPS

SIZES OF CROCK-POT® SLOW COOKERS

Smaller **CROCK-POT**® slow cookers—such as 1- to 3½-quart models—are the perfect size for cooking for singles, a couple or empty nesters (and also for serving dips).

While medium-size **CROCK-POT**® slow cookers (those holding between 3 quarts and 5 quarts) will easily cook enough food at one time to feed a small family, they are also convenient for holiday side dishes or appetizers.

Large **CROCK-POT**® slow cookers are great for large family dinners, holiday entertaining and potluck suppers. A 6- to 7-quart model is ideal if you like to make meals in advance. Or, have dinner tonight and store leftovers for later.

TYPES OF CROCK-POT® SLOW COOKERS

Current **CROCK-POT**® slow cookers come equipped with many different features and benefits, from auto cook programs to oven-safe stoneware to timed programming. Please visit **WWW.CROCK-POT.COM** to find the **CROCK-POT**® slow cooker that best suits your needs.

How you plan to use a **CROCK-POT**® slow cooker may affect the model you choose to purchase. For everyday cooking, choose a size large enough to serve your family. If you plan to use the **CROCK-POT**® slow cooker primarily for entertaining, choose one of the larger sizes. Basic **CROCK-POT**® slow cookers can hold as little as 16 ounces or as much as 7 quarts. The smallest sizes are great for keeping dips warm on a buffet, while the larger sizes can more readily fit large quantities of food and larger roasts.

COOKING, STIRRING AND FOOD SAFETY

CROCK-POT® slow cookers are safe to leave unattended. The outer heating base may get hot as it cooks, but it should not pose a fire hazard. The heating element in the heating base functions at a low wattage and is safe for your countertops.

Your **CROCK-POT**® slow cooker should be filled about one-half to three-fourths full for most recipes unless otherwise instructed. Lean meats such as chicken or pork tenderloin will cook faster than meats with more connective tissue and fat such as beef chuck or pork shoulder. Bone-in meats will take longer than boneless cuts. Typical **CROCK-POT**® slow cooker dishes take approximately 7 to 8 hours to reach the simmer point on LOW and about 3 to 4 hours on HIGH. Once the vegetables and meat start to simmer and braise, their flavors will fully blend and meat will become fall-off-the-bone tender.

According to the U.S. Department of Agriculture, all bacteria are killed at a temperature of 165°F. It's important to follow the recommended cooking times and not to open the lid often, especially early in the cooking process when heat is building up inside the unit. If you need to open the lid to check on your food or are adding additional ingredients, remember to allow additional cooking time if necessary to ensure food is cooked through and tender.

Large **CROCK-POT**® slow cookers, the 6- to 7-quart sizes, may benefit from a quick stir halfway through cook time to help distribute heat and promote even cooking. It's usually unnecessary to stir at all, as even ½ cup liquid will help to distribute heat, and the stoneware is the perfect medium for holding food at an even temperature throughout the cooking process.

OVEN-SAFE STONEWARE

All **CROCK-POT**® slow cooker removable stoneware inserts may (without their lids) be used safely in ovens at up to 400°F. In addition, all **CROCK-POT**® slow cookers are microwavable without their lids. If you own another slow cooker brand, please refer to your owner's manual for specific stoneware cooking medium tolerances.

FROZEN FOOD

Frozen food can be successfully cooked in a **CROCK-POT**® slow cooker. However, it will require longer cooking time than the same recipe made with fresh food. Using an instant-read thermometer is recommended to ensure meat is fully cooked.

Macaroni and Cheese
p. 127

PASTA AND RICE

If you are converting a recipe for your **CROCK-POT**® slow cooker that calls for uncooked pasta, first cook the pasta on the stovetop just until slightly tender. Then add the pasta to the **CROCK-POT**® slow cooker.

If you are converting a recipe for the **CROCK-POT**® slow cooker that calls for cooked rice, stir in raw rice with the other recipe ingredients plus ¼ cup extra liquid per ¼ cup of raw rice.

BEANS

Beans must be softened completely before combining with sugar and/or acidic foods in the **CROCK-POT**® slow cooker. Sugar and acid have a hardening effect on beans and will prevent softening. Fully cooked canned beans may be used as a substitute for dried beans.

VEGETABLES

Root vegetables often cook more slowly than meat. Cut vegetables accordingly to cook at the same rate as meat—large versus small or lean versus marbled—and place near the sides or bottom of the stoneware to facilitate cooking.

HERBS

Fresh herbs add flavor and color when added at the end of the cooking cycle; if added at the beginning, many fresh herbs' flavor will dissipate over long cook times. Ground and/or dried herbs and spices work well in slow cooking and may be added at the beginning of cook time. For dishes with shorter cook times, hearty fresh herbs such as rosemary and thyme hold up well. The flavor power of all herbs and spices can vary greatly depending on their particular strength and shelf life. Use chili powders and garlic powder sparingly, as these can sometimes intensify over the long cook times. Always taste the finished dish and correct seasonings including salt and pepper.

LIQUIDS

It is not necessary to use more than ½ to 1 cup liquid in most instances. Most juices in meats and vegetables are retained more in slow cooking than in conventional cooking. Excess liquid can be cooked down and concentrated after slow cooking, either the stovetop or by removing the meat and vegetables from the stoneware. Then stir in one of the following thickeners and set the **CROCK-POT**® slow cooker to HIGH. Cover and cook the liquid on HIGH for approximately 15 minutes or until thickened.

FLOUR: All-purpose flour is often used to thicken soups or stews. Stir water into the flour in a small bowl until smooth. With the **CROCK-POT**® slow cooker on HIGH, whisk flour mixture into the liquid in the **CROCK-POT**® slow cooker. Cover; cook on HIGH 15 minutes or until the mixture is thickened.

CORNSTARCH: Cornstarch gives sauces a clear, shiny appearance; it's used most often for sweet dessert sauces and stir-fry sauces. Stir water into the cornstarch in a small bowl until the cornstarch is dissolved. Quickly stir this mixture into the liquid in the **CROCK-POT**® slow cooker; the sauce will thicken as soon as the liquid simmers. Cornstarch breaks down with too much heat, so never add it at the beginning of the slow cooking process and turn off the heat as soon as the sauce thickens.

MILK

Milk, cream and sour cream break down during extended cooking. When possible, add them during the last 15 to 30 minutes of slow cooking, until just heated through. Condensed soups may be substituted for milk and may cook for extended times.

FISH

Fish is delicate and should be stirred into the **CROCK-POT**® slow cooker gently during the last 15 to 30 minutes of cooking. Cover; cook just until cooked through and serve immediately.

BAKED GOODS

If you wish to prepare bread, cakes or pudding cakes in a **CROCK-POT**® slow cooker, you may want to purchase a covered, vented metal cake pan accessory for your **CROCK-POT**® slow cooker. You can also use any straight-sided soufflé dish or deep cake pan that will fit into the stoneware of your unit. Baked goods can be prepared directly in the stoneware; however, they can be a little difficult to remove from the insert, so follow the recipe directions carefully.

Vanilla Sour Cream
Cheesecake
p. 166

TRIED-AND-TRUE BREAKFAST

MAPLE, BACON AND RASPBERRY PANCAKE

MAKES 8 SERVINGS

5 slices bacon

2 cups pancake mix

1 cup water

½ cup maple syrup, plus additional for serving

1 cup fresh raspberries, plus additional for garnish

3 tablespoons chopped pecans, toasted*

To toast pecans, spread in single layer in heavy skillet. Cook and stir over medium heat 1 to 2 minutes or until nuts are lightly browned.

1. Heat large skillet over medium heat. Add bacon; cook and stir until crisp. Remove to paper towel-lined plate using slotted spoon; crumble.

2. Brush inside of 5-quart **CROCK-POT**® slow cooker with 1 to 2 tablespoons bacon fat from skillet. Combine pancake mix, water and ½ cup maple syrup in large bowl; stir to blend. Pour half of batter into **CROCK-POT**® slow cooker; top with ½ cup raspberries, half of bacon and half of pecans. Pour remaining half of batter over top; sprinkle with remaining ½ cup raspberries, bacon and pecans.

3. Cover; cook on HIGH 1½ to 2 hours or until pancake has risen and is cooked through. Turn off heat. Let stand, uncovered, 10 to 15 minutes. Remove pancake from **CROCK-POT**® slow cooker; cut into eight pieces. Serve with additional maple syrup and raspberries.

WAKE-UP POTATO AND SAUSAGE BREAKFAST CASSEROLE

MAKES 8 SERVINGS

1 pound kielbasa or smoked sausage, diced

1 cup chopped onion

1 cup chopped red bell pepper

1 package (20 ounces) refrigerated southwest-style hash browns*

10 eggs

1 cup milk

1 cup (4 ounces) shredded Monterey Jack or sharp Cheddar cheese

*You may substitute O'Brien potatoes and add ½ teaspoon chile pepper.

1. Coat inside of **CROCK-POT**® slow cooker with nonstick cooking spray. Heat large skillet over medium-high heat. Add sausage and onion; cook and stir until sausage is browned. Drain fat. Stir in bell pepper.

2. Place one third of potatoes in **CROCK-POT**® slow cooker. Top with half of sausage mixture. Repeat layers. Spread remaining one third of potatoes evenly on top.

3. Whisk eggs and milk in medium bowl. Pour evenly over potatoes. Cover; cook on LOW 6 to 7 hours.

4. Turn off heat. Sprinkle cheese over casserole; let stand 10 minutes or until cheese is melted.

MAPLE PUMPKIN BUTTER

MAKES 4 CUPS

- 2 cans (about 15 ounces *each*) pumpkin purée
- ¾ cup packed dark brown sugar
- ¼ cup maple syrup
- 2 teaspoons ground cinnamon
- ½ teaspoon ground ginger
- ¼ teaspoon ground cloves
- ¼ teaspoon ground allspice
- ¼ teaspoon ground nutmeg
- ⅛ teaspoon salt
- 1 tablespoon lemon juice

1. Combine pumpkin purée, brown sugar, maple syrup, cinnamon, ginger, cloves, allspice, nutmeg and salt in **CROCK-POT**® slow cooker; stir to blend. Cover; cook on LOW 7 hours or on HIGH 3½ hours, stirring every 2 to 3 hours.

2. Stir in lemon juice. Divide among storage containers; cool completely. Cover; refrigerate up to 3 weeks.

PEAR CRUNCH

MAKES 4 SERVINGS

- 1 can (8 ounces) crushed pineapple in juice, undrained
- ¼ cup pineapple or apple juice
- 3 tablespoons dried cranberries
- 1½ teaspoons quick-cooking tapioca
- ¼ teaspoon vanilla
- 2 pears, cored and halved
- ¼ cup granola with almonds

1. Combine pineapple, pineapple juice, cranberries, tapioca and vanilla in **CROCK-POT**® slow cooker; stir to blend. Top with pears, cut sides down.

2. Cover; cook on LOW 3½ to 4½ hours. Arrange pear halves on serving plates. Spoon pineapple mixture over pear halves. Sprinkle with granola.

Maple Pumpkin Butter

BREAKFAST BERRY BREAD PUDDING

MAKES 10 TO 12 SERVINGS

6 cups bread, preferably dense peasant-style or sourdough, cut into ¾- to 1-inch cubes

1 cup raisins

½ cup slivered almonds, toasted*

6 eggs, beaten

1½ cups packed light brown sugar

1¾ cups milk

1½ teaspoons ground cinnamon

1 teaspoon vanilla

3 cups sliced fresh strawberries

2 cups fresh blueberries

Fresh mint leaves (optional)

*To toast almonds, spread in single layer in heavy skillet. Cook and stir over medium heat 1 to 2 minutes or until nuts are lightly browned.

1. Coat inside of **CROCK-POT**® slow cooker with nonstick cooking spray or butter. Add bread, raisins and almonds; toss to combine.

2. Whisk eggs, brown sugar, milk, cinnamon and vanilla in separate bowl. Pour egg mixture over bread mixture; toss to blend. Cover; cook on LOW 4 to 4½ hours or on HIGH 3 hours.

3. Remove stoneware from **CROCK-POT**® base and allow bread pudding to cool and set before serving. Serve with berries and garnish with mint leaves.

OVERNIGHT BACON, SOURDOUGH, EGG AND CHEESE CASSEROLE

MAKES 6 SERVINGS

1 loaf (about 12 ounces) sourdough bread, cut into ¾-inch cubes

8 slices thick-cut bacon, chopped

1 large onion, chopped

1 medium red bell pepper, chopped

1 medium green bell pepper, chopped

2 teaspoons dried oregano

¼ cup sun-dried tomatoes packed in oil, drained and chopped

1½ cups (6 ounces) shredded sharp Cheddar cheese, divided

10 eggs

1 cup milk

1 teaspoon salt

¾ teaspoon black pepper

1. Coat inside of **CROCK-POT®** slow cooker with nonstick cooking spray. Place bread in **CROCK-POT®** slow cooker. Heat large skillet over medium heat. Add bacon; cook 7 to 9 minutes or until crisp. Remove bacon to paper towel-lined plate, using slotted spoon. Pour off all but 1 tablespoon of drippings from skillet. Heat same skillet over medium heat. Add onion, bell peppers and oregano; cook 2 to 3 minutes or until onion is softened, stirring occasionally. Stir in sun-dried tomatoes; cook 1 minute. Pour over bread in **CROCK-POT®** slow cooker. Stir in bacon and 1 cup cheese.

2. Beat eggs, milk, salt and black pepper in large bowl; pour over bread mixture in **CROCK-POT®** slow cooker. Press down on bread to allow bread mixture to absorb egg mixture. Sprinkle remaining ½ cup cheese over top. Cover; cook on LOW 6 to 8 hours or on HIGH 3½ to 4 hours. Cut into squares to serve.

APPLE AND GRANOLA BREAKFAST COBBLER

MAKES 4 SERVINGS

4 Granny Smith apples, peeled, cored and sliced

½ cup packed light brown sugar

1 tablespoon lemon juice

1 teaspoon ground cinnamon

2 cups granola cereal, plus additional for garnish

2 tablespoons butter, cut into small pieces

Whipping cream, half-and-half or vanilla yogurt (optional)

1. Place apples in **CROCK-POT**® slow cooker. Sprinkle brown sugar, lemon juice and cinnamon over apples. Stir in 2 cups granola and butter.

2. Cover; cook on LOW 6 hours or on HIGH 3 hours. Serve warm with additional granola sprinkled on top. Serve with cream, if desired.

⭐ **TIP:** Granny Smith apples are crisp, tart and juicy. They are an excellent choice for pies, cobblers and crisps. Jonagold, Golden Delicious and the more recently available, Cameo, are good substitutes.

ROASTED PEPPER AND SOURDOUGH EGG DISH

MAKES 6 SERVINGS

- 3 cups sourdough bread cubes
- 1 jar (12 ounces) roasted red pepper strips, drained
- 1 cup (4 ounces) shredded Monterey Jack cheese
- 1 cup (4 ounces) shredded sharp Cheddar cheese
- 1 cup cottage cheese
- 6 eggs
- 1 cup milk
- ¼ cup chopped fresh cilantro
- ¼ teaspoon black pepper

1. Coat inside of **CROCK-POT®** slow cooker with nonstick cooking spray. Add bread. Arrange roasted peppers evenly over bread cubes; sprinkle with Monterey Jack and Cheddar cheeses.

2. Place cottage cheese in food processor or blender; process until smooth. Add eggs and milk; process just until blended. Stir in cilantro and black pepper.

3. Pour egg mixture into **CROCK-POT®** slow cooker. Cover; cook on LOW 3 to 3½ hours or on HIGH 2 to 2½ hours or until eggs are firm but still moist.

BACON AND CHEESE BRUNCH POTATOES

MAKES 6 SERVINGS

3 medium russet potatoes (about 2 pounds), peeled and cut into 1-inch cubes

1 cup chopped onion

½ teaspoon seasoned salt

4 slices bacon, crisp-cooked and crumbled

1 cup (4 ounces) shredded sharp Cheddar cheese

1 tablespoon water

1. Coat inside of **CROCK-POT**® slow cooker with nonstick cooking spray. Place half of potatoes in **CROCK-POT**® slow cooker. Sprinkle half of onion and seasoned salt over potatoes; top with half of bacon and cheese. Repeat layers. Sprinkle water over top.

2. Cover; cook on LOW 6 hours or on HIGH 3½ hours or until potatoes and onion are tender. Stir gently to mix; serve warm.

⭐ **TIP:** To microwave bacon, place slices, without overlapping, in a single layer between paper towels on a microwavable rack or plate. Microwave on HIGH about 1 minute per slice. Be careful when removing cooked bacon from the microwave because the bacon grease can get extremely hot.

OVERNIGHT BREAKFAST PORRIDGE

MAKES 4 SERVINGS

¾ cup steel-cut oats

¼ cup uncooked quinoa, rinsed and drained

¼ cup dried cranberries, plus additional for serving

¼ cup raisins

3 tablespoons ground flax seeds

2 tablespoons chia seeds

¼ teaspoon ground cinnamon

2½ cups almond milk, plus additional for serving

Maple syrup (optional)

¼ cup sliced almonds, toasted*

To toast almonds, spread in single layer in heavy skillet. Cook and stir over medium heat 1 to 2 minutes or until nuts are lightly browned.

1. Combine oats, quinoa, ¼ cup cranberries, raisins, flax seeds, chia seeds and cinnamon in heat-safe bowl that fits inside of 5- or 6-quart **CROCK-POT**® slow cooker. Stir in 2½ cups almond milk.

2. Place bowl in **CROCK-POT**® slow cooker; pour enough water to come halfway up side of bowl.

3. Cover; cook on LOW 8 hours. Carefully remove bowl from **CROCK-POT**® slow cooker. Stir in additional almond milk. Top each serving with maple syrup, almonds and additional cranberries, if desired.

SAVORY SAUSAGE BREAD PUDDING

MAKES 4 TO 6 SERVINGS

4 eggs

2 cups milk *or* 1 cup *each* half-and-half and milk

¼ teaspoon salt

¼ teaspoon black pepper

¼ teaspoon dried thyme

⅛ teaspoon red pepper flakes

1 package (10 ounces) smoked breakfast sausage links, cut into ½-inch pieces

¾ cup (3 ounces) shredded Cheddar cheese

2 cups day-old bread, cut into ½-inch cubes

1. Beat eggs in large bowl. Stir in milk, salt, black pepper, thyme and red pepper flakes. Add sausage, cheese and bread; press bread into egg mixture. Let stand 10 minutes or until liquid is absorbed.

2. Generously butter 2-quart baking dish that fits inside of **CROCK-POT**® slow cooker. Pour sausage mixture into baking dish. Cover dish with buttered foil, butter side down.

3. Pour 1 inch hot water into **CROCK-POT**® slow cooker. Add baking dish. Cover; cook on LOW 4 to 5 hours or until toothpick inserted into center comes out clean.

WHEAT AND WALNUT LOAF

MAKES 1 LOAF

2 cups warm water (100°F to 110°F), divided

¼ cup sugar

2 tablespoons vegetable oil

1 packet (¼ ounce) active dry yeast

2 cups all-purpose flour

1 cup whole wheat flour

⅔ cup walnut halves and pieces

1½ teaspoons salt

1. Combine 1 cup water, sugar, oil and yeast in small bowl; mix well. Let stand 5 minutes.

2. Combine flours, walnuts and salt in large bowl; stir to blend. Pour yeast mixture over flour mixture; stir until rough dough forms. Turn dough out onto floured surface; knead 6 to 7 minutes or until smooth and elastic. Place in 2½-quart ceramic baking dish. Cover with plastic wrap; let stand in warm place 30 minutes.

3. Place crumpled foil in bottom of 6-quart oval **CROCK-POT**® slow cooker. Pour in remaining 1 cup water. Remove plastic wrap from baking dish. Carefully place baking dish in **CROCK-POT**® slow cooker.

4. Cover; cook on HIGH 2¾ to 3 hours or until bread is cooked through and pulls away from sides. Remove bread from baking dish; let cool on wire rack 30 minutes.

HASH BROWN AND SPINACH BREAKFAST CASSEROLE

MAKES 6 TO 8 SERVINGS

4 cups frozen southern-style diced hash browns

3 tablespoons unsalted butter

1 large onion, chopped

2 cups (8 ounces) sliced mushrooms

3 cloves garlic, minced

1 package (10 ounces) frozen chopped spinach, thawed and squeezed dry

8 eggs

1 cup milk

1 teaspoon salt

¼ teaspoon black pepper

1½ cups (6 ounces) shredded sharp Cheddar cheese, divided

1. Coat inside of **CROCK-POT®** slow cooker with nonstick cooking spray. Place hash browns in **CROCK-POT®** slow cooker.

2. Melt butter in large skillet over medium-high heat. Add onion, mushrooms and garlic; cook 4 to 5 minutes or until onion is just starting to brown, stirring occasionally. Add spinach; cook 2 minutes or until mushrooms are tender. Stir spinach mixture into **CROCK-POT®** slow cooker with hash browns until combined.

3. Combine eggs, milk, salt and pepper in large bowl; mix well. Pour over hash brown mixture in **CROCK-POT®** slow cooker. Top with 1 cup cheese. Cover; cook on LOW 4 to 4½ hours or on HIGH 1½ to 2 hours or until eggs are set. Top with remaining ½ cup cheese. Cut into wedges to serve.

HAWAIIAN FRUIT COMPOTE

MAKES 6 TO 8 SERVINGS

3 cups coarsely chopped
   fresh pineapple

3 grapefruits, peeled and
   sectioned

1 can (21 ounces) cherry pie
   filling

2 cups chopped fresh peaches

2 to 3 limes, peeled and
   sectioned

1 mango, peeled and
   chopped

2 bananas, sliced

1 tablespoon lemon juice

Slivered almonds (optional)

Combine pineapple, grapefruits, pie filling, peaches, limes, mango, bananas and lemon juice in **CROCK-POT®** slow cooker; toss to blend. Cover; cook on LOW 4 to 5 hours or on HIGH 2 to 3 hours. Sprinkle with almonds, if desired.

FOUR FRUIT OATMEAL

MAKES 4 SERVINGS

4¼ cups water

1 cup steel-cut oats

⅓ cup golden raisins

⅓ cup dried cranberries

⅓ cup dried cherries

2 tablespoons honey

1 teaspoon vanilla

¼ teaspoon salt

1 cup fresh sliced strawberries

Combine water, oats, raisins, cranberries, cherries, honey, vanilla and salt in **CROCK-POT®** slow cooker; stir well. Cover; cook on LOW 7 to 7½ hours. Top each serving evenly with strawberries.

Hawaiian Fruit Compote

BREAKFAST BAKE

MAKES 6 TO 8 SERVINGS

3 to 4 cups diced crusty bread (¾- to 1-inch dice)

½ pound bacon, cut into ½-inch dice

2 cups sliced mushrooms

2 cups torn fresh spinach

8 eggs

½ cup milk

1 cup (4 ounces) shredded Cheddar or Monterey Jack cheese

¾ cup roasted red peppers, drained and chopped

Salt and black pepper

1. Coat inside of **CROCK-POT®** slow cooker with nonstick cooking spray. Add bread.

2. Heat large skillet over medium heat. Add bacon; cook and stir until crisp. Remove to **CROCK-POT®** slow cooker using slotted spoon. Discard all but 1 tablespoon drippings. Add mushrooms and spinach to skillet; cook and stir 1 to 2 minutes or until spinach is wilted. Remove to **CROCK-POT®** slow cooker; toss to combine.

3. Beat eggs and milk in medium bowl. Stir in cheese and red peppers. Season with salt and black pepper. Pour into **CROCK-POT®** slow cooker. Cover; cook on LOW 3 to 3½ hours or on HIGH 2 to 2½ hours or until eggs are firm but still moist.

SPARKLING APPETIZERS

RASPBERRY BBQ CHICKEN WINGS

MAKES 5 TO 6 SERVINGS

3 pounds chicken drummettes and wings, tips removed and split at joints

¾ cup seedless raspberry jam

½ cup sweet and tangy prepared barbecue sauce

1 tablespoon raspberry red wine vinegar

1 teaspoon chili powder

1. Coat inside of **CROCK-POT**® slow cooker with nonstick cooking spray. Preheat broiler. Spray large baking sheet with cooking spray. Arrange chicken on prepared baking sheet. Broil 6 to 8 minutes until browned, turning once. Remove to **CROCK-POT**® slow cooker.

2. Combine jam, barbecue sauce, vinegar and chili powder in medium bowl; stir to blend. Pour sauce over chicken in **CROCK-POT**® slow cooker; turn to coat. Cover; cook on LOW 3½ to 4 hours. Remove chicken to large serving platter; cover to keep warm.

3. Turn **CROCK-POT**® slow cooker to HIGH. Cook, uncovered, on HIGH 10 to 15 minutes or until sauce is thickened. Spoon sauce over chicken to serve.

BACON-WRAPPED FINGERLING POTATOES

MAKES 4 TO 6 SERVINGS

1 pound fingerling potatoes

2 tablespoons olive oil

1 tablespoon minced fresh thyme

½ teaspoon black pepper

¼ teaspoon paprika

½ pound bacon slices, cut crosswise into halves

¼ cup chicken broth

Sprigs fresh thyme (optional)

1. Toss potatoes with oil, minced thyme, pepper and paprika in large bowl. Wrap half slice of bacon tightly around each potato.

2. Heat large skillet over medium heat; add potatoes. Reduce heat to medium-low; cook until lightly browned and bacon has tightened around potatoes. Place potatoes in **CROCK-POT**® slow cooker. Add broth. Cover; cook on HIGH 3 hours. Garnish with thyme sprigs.

⭐ **TIP:** Bacon will keep in the refrigerator about 10 days or can be frozen for up to 3 months.

PARTY MIX

MAKES 10 CUPS

3 cups rice squares cereal

2 cups toasted oat ring cereal

2 cups wheat squares cereal

1 cup pistachio nuts or peanuts

1 cup thin pretzel sticks

½ cup (1 stick) butter, melted

1 tablespoon Worcestershire sauce

1 teaspoon seasoned salt

½ teaspoon garlic powder

⅛ teaspoon ground red pepper (optional)

1. Combine cereals, nuts and pretzels in **CROCK-POT®** slow cooker.

2. Combine butter, Worcestershire sauce, seasoned salt, garlic powder and ground red pepper, if desired, in small bowl; stir to blend. Pour over cereal mixture in **CROCK-POT®** slow cooker; toss lightly to coat.

3. Cover; cook on LOW 3 hours, stirring well every 30 minutes. Cook, uncovered, on LOW 30 minutes. Store in airtight container.

PULLED PORK SLIDERS WITH COLA BARBECUE SAUCE

MAKES 16 SLIDERS

1 teaspoon vegetable oil

1 boneless pork shoulder roast (3 pounds)*

1 cup cola

¼ cup tomato paste

2 tablespoons packed brown sugar

2 teaspoons Worcestershire sauce

2 teaspoons spicy brown mustard

Hot pepper sauce

Salt

16 dinner rolls or potato rolls, split

Sliced pickles (optional)

Unless you have a 5-, 6- or 7-quart CROCK-POT® slow cooker, cut any roast larger than 2½ pounds in half so it cooks completely.

1. Heat oil in large skillet over medium-high heat. Add pork; cook 6 to 8 minutes or until browned on all sides. Remove to **CROCK-POT**® slow cooker. Pour cola over pork. Cover; cook on LOW 7½ to 8 hours or on HIGH 3½ to 4 hours.

2. Turn off heat. Remove pork to large cutting board; shred with two forks. Let cooking liquid stand 5 minutes. Skim off and discard fat. Whisk tomato paste, brown sugar, Worcestershire sauce and mustard into cooking liquid. Cover; cook on HIGH 15 minutes or until thickened.

3. Stir shredded pork back into **CROCK-POT**® slow cooker. Season with hot pepper sauce and salt. Serve on rolls. Top with pickles, if desired.

HONEY-GLAZED CHICKEN WINGS

MAKES 6 SERVINGS

3 tablespoons vegetable oil, divided

3 pounds chicken wings

1 cup honey

½ cup soy sauce

2 tablespoons tomato paste

2 teaspoons water

1 clove garlic, minced

1 teaspoon sugar

1 teaspoon black pepper

1. Heat 1½ tablespoons oil in large skillet over medium heat. Add wings in batches; cook 1 to 2 minutes on each side or until browned. Remove to **CROCK-POT®** slow cooker using slotted spoon.

2. Combine remaining 1½ tablespoons oil, honey, soy sauce, tomato paste, water, garlic, sugar and pepper in medium bowl; stir to blend. Pour sauce over wings. Cover; cook on LOW 6 to 8 hours or on HIGH 3 to 4 hours.

PARTY MEATBALLS

MAKES 10 TO 12 SERVINGS

1 package (about 1 pound) frozen cocktail-size beef meatballs

½ cup maple syrup

1 jar (12 ounces) chili sauce

1 jar (12 ounces) grape jelly

Place meatballs, maple syrup, chili sauce and jelly in **CROCK-POT®** slow cooker; stir to blend. Cover; cook on LOW 3 to 4 hours or on HIGH 2 to 3 hours.

BARBECUE BEEF SLIDERS

MAKES 6 SERVINGS

1 tablespoon packed light brown sugar

1 teaspoon ground cumin

1 teaspoon chili powder

1 teaspoon paprika

½ teaspoon salt

¼ teaspoon ground red pepper

3 pounds beef short ribs

½ cup plus 2 tablespoons barbecue sauce, divided

¼ cup water

12 slider rolls

¾ cup prepared coleslaw

12 bread and butter pickle chips

1. Coat inside of **CROCK-POT®** slow cooker with nonstick cooking spray. Combine brown sugar, cumin, chili powder, paprika, salt and ground red pepper in small bowl; toss to blend. Rub over ribs; remove to **CROCK-POT®** slow cooker. Pour in ½ cup barbecue sauce and water; toss to coat ribs.

2. Cover; cook on LOW 7 to 8 hours or on HIGH 4 to 4½ hours or until ribs are very tender and meat shreds easily. Remove ribs to large cutting board. Discard bones; remove meat to large bowl. Shred meat using two forks, discarding any large pieces of fat. Stir in remaining 2 tablespoons barbecue sauce and 2 tablespoons liquid from **CROCK-POT®** slow cooker.

3. Arrange bottom half of rolls on platter or work surface. Top each with ¼ cup beef mixture, 1 tablespoon coleslaw and 1 pickle chip. Place roll tops on each.

BRATS IN BEER

MAKES 30 TO 36 APPETIZERS

1½ pounds bratwurst (5 to 6 links)

1 can (12 ounces) amber ale or beer

1 onion, thinly sliced

2 tablespoons packed brown sugar

2 tablespoons red wine vinegar or cider vinegar

Spicy brown mustard

Cocktail rye bread

1. Combine bratwurst, ale, onion, brown sugar and vinegar in **CROCK-POT®** slow cooker. Cover; cook on LOW 4 to 5 hours.

2. Remove bratwurst from cooking liquid. Cut into ½-inch-thick slices.

3. Spread mustard on cocktail rye bread. Top with bratwurst slices and onion.

⭐ **TIP:** Beer is a low-alcohol beverage made by malting cereals (principally barley), adding flavor with hops and then fermenting the mixture. Yeast is added to start the fermentation process, which results in alcohol and carbon dioxide. The carbon dioxide, which is not allowed to escape, results in the characteristic fizz. Since beer has a high percentage of water, the quality or the source of the water plays a major role in the flavor and character of beer. There are many types of beer including lager, light, ale, stout and porter.

HOT SAUCE DRUMMETTES

MAKES 8 SERVINGS

4 pounds chicken wing drummettes

2 teaspoons creole seasoning

⅛ teaspoon black pepper

2½ cups hot pepper sauce

¼ cup vegetable oil

¼ cup vinegar

4 teaspoons honey

1 teaspoon red pepper flakes

1 cup blue cheese dressing

Fresh celery stalks

1. Preheat broiler. Place drummettes on rack in broiler pan; season with creole seasoning and black pepper. Broil 4 to 5 inches from heat 10 to 12 minutes or until browned, turning once. Remove drummettes to **CROCK-POT**® slow cooker using tongs.

2. Combine hot pepper sauce, oil, vinegar, honey and red pepper flakes in medium bowl; stir to blend. Pour over drummettes. Cover; cook on LOW 5 to 6 hours. Serve with dressing and celery.

SAUCED LITTLE SMOKIES

MAKES 24 SERVINGS

1 bottle (14 ounces) barbecue sauce

¾ cup grape jelly

½ cup packed brown sugar

½ cup ketchup

1 tablespoon prepared mustard

1 teaspoon Worcestershire sauce

3 packages (14 to 16 ounces *each*) miniature cocktail franks

Stir barbecue sauce, jelly, brown sugar, ketchup, mustard and Worcestershire sauce into **CROCK-POT**® slow cooker until combined. Add cocktail franks; stir to coat. Cover; cook on LOW 3 to 4 hours or on HIGH 1 to 2 hours.

ANGELIC DEVILED EGGS

MAKES 12 SERVINGS

6 eggs

¼ cup cottage cheese

3 tablespoons ranch dressing

2 teaspoons Dijon mustard

2 tablespoons minced fresh chives or dill

1 tablespoon diced well-drained pimientos or roasted red pepper

1. Place eggs in single layer in bottom of **CROCK-POT**® slow cooker; add just enough water to cover tops of eggs. Cover; cook on LOW 3½ hours. Rinse and drain eggs under cold running water; peel when cool enough to handle.

2. Cut eggs in half lengthwise. Remove yolks, reserving 3 yolk halves. Discard remaining yolks or reserve for another use. Place egg whites, cut sides up, on serving plate; cover with plastic wrap. Refrigerate while preparing filling.

3. Combine cottage cheese, dressing, mustard and reserved yolk halves in small bowl; mash with fork until well blended. Stir in chives and pimientos. Spoon cottage cheese mixture into egg whites. Cover; refrigerate at least 1 hour before serving.

SUPER MEATBALL SLIDERS

MAKES 24 SLIDERS

1 can (15 ounces) whole berry cranberry sauce

1 can (about 15 ounces) tomato sauce

⅛ teaspoon red pepper flakes (optional)

2 pounds ground beef or turkey

¾ cup seasoned dry bread crumbs

1 egg, lightly beaten

1 package (1 ounce) onion soup mix

Baby arugula leaves (optional)

24 small potato rolls or dinner rolls, split

6 slices (1 ounce *each*) provolone cheese, cut into quarters

1. Combine cranberry sauce, tomato sauce and red pepper flakes, if desired, in **CROCK-POT®** slow cooker; stir to blend. Cover; cook on LOW 3 to 4 hours.

2. Halfway through cooking time, prepare meatballs. Combine beef, bread crumbs, egg and dry soup mix in large bowl; mix well. Shape mixture into 24 meatballs (about 1¾ inches diameter). Spray large skillet with nonstick cooking spray; heat over medium heat. Add meatballs; cook 8 to 10 minutes or until browned on all sides. Remove to **CROCK-POT®** slow cooker.

3. Cover; cook on LOW 1 to 2 hours. Place arugula leaves on bottom of rolls, if desired. Top with meatballs, sauce, cheese and tops of rolls.

LEMON AND GARLIC SHRIMP

MAKES 6 TO 8 SERVINGS

1 pound large raw shrimp, peeled and deveined (with tails on)

½ cup (1 stick) unsalted butter, cubed

3 cloves garlic, crushed

2 tablespoons lemon juice

½ teaspoon paprika

Salt and black pepper

2 tablespoons finely chopped fresh Italian parsley

1. Coat inside of **CROCK-POT**® slow cooker with nonstick cooking spray. Add shrimp, butter and garlic; mix well. Cover; cook on HIGH 1¼ hours.

2. Turn off heat. Stir in lemon juice, paprika, salt and pepper. Spoon shrimp and liquid into serving bowls; sprinkle with parsley.

BACON-WRAPPED SCALLOPS

MAKES 12 SERVINGS

24 sea scallops, side muscle removed

½ cup Belgian white ale

3 tablespoons chopped fresh cilantro

2 tablespoons honey

¼ teaspoon chipotle chili powder

12 slices bacon, halved

1. Pour ½ inch of water in bottom of **CROCK-POT®** slow cooker. Combine scallops, ale, cilantro, honey and chipotle chili powder in medium bowl; toss to coat. Refrigerate 30 minutes.

2. Place 1 scallop on end of 1 bacon half. Roll up jelly-roll style and secure with toothpick. Remove to large baking sheet. Repeat with remaining bacon and scallops. Brush tops of scallops with ale mixture.

3. Heat large skillet over medium heat. Add wrapped scallops; cook 5 to 7 minutes or until bacon is just beginning to brown. Remove to **CROCK-POT®** slow cooker. Cover; cook on LOW 1 hour.

PEPPERONI PIZZA DIP

MAKES 1⅓ CUPS

Easy Breadsticks (recipe follows) or other prepared breadsticks

1 jar (about 14 ounces) pizza sauce

⅓ cup chopped pepperoni

½ can (about 2¼ ounces) sliced black olives, drained

1 teaspoon dried oregano

¼ cup (1 ounce) shredded mozzarella cheese

½ package (about 1½ ounces) cream cheese, softened

1 tablespoon olive oil

1. Prepare Easy Breadsticks. Combine pizza sauce, pepperoni, olives and oregano in medium saucepan; stir to blend. Bring to a boil over medium-high heat, stirring frequently. Reduce heat to low. Stir in mozzarella cheese and cream cheese until melted. Remove from heat and stir in oil.

2. Coat inside of **CROCK-POT®** "No Dial" food warmer with nonstick cooking spray. Fill with dip to keep warm. Serve with Easy Breadsticks.

EASY BREADSTICKS: Preheat oven to 400°F. Grease baking sheets or line with parchment paper. Unroll 1 package (10 ounces) refrigerated pizza dough on lightly floured work surface. Shape dough into 16×10-inch rectangle. Brush with melted butter. Cut into 24 (10-inch) strips. Form into desired shape. Place breadsticks ½ inch apart on prepared baking sheets. Bake 10 minutes or until golden brown. Sprinkle with 2 tablespoons dried oregano. Serve immediately or place on wire rack to cool.

BARBECUED MEATBALLS

MAKES ABOUT 4 DOZEN

2 pounds ground beef

1⅓ cups ketchup, divided

3 tablespoons seasoned dry bread crumbs

1 egg, lightly beaten

2 tablespoons dried minced onion

¾ teaspoon garlic salt

½ teaspoon black pepper

1 cup packed brown sugar

1 can (6 ounces) tomato paste

¼ cup soy sauce

¼ cup cider vinegar

1½ teaspoons hot pepper sauce

Sliced green bell peppers

1. Preheat oven to 350°F. Combine beef, ⅓ cup ketchup, bread crumbs, egg, dried onion, garlic salt and black pepper in large bowl; mix well. Shape into 1-inch meatballs.

2. Place meatballs in two 15×10-inch jelly-roll pans or shallow roasting pans. Bake 18 minutes or until browned. Remove to **CROCK-POT**® slow cooker using slotted spoon.

3. Combine remaining 1 cup ketchup, brown sugar, tomato paste, soy sauce, vinegar and hot pepper sauce in medium bowl; stir to blend. Pour over meatballs. Cover; cook on LOW 4 hours. Stir in bell peppers during last 15 minutes of cooking.

JUICY REUBEN SLIDERS

MAKES 24 SLIDERS

1 corned beef brisket (about 1½ pounds), trimmed

2 cups sauerkraut, drained

½ cup beef broth

1 small onion, sliced

1 clove garlic, minced

4 to 6 whole white peppercorns

¼ teaspoon caraway seeds

48 slices cocktail rye bread or pumpernickel

12 slices deli Swiss cheese

Dijon mustard (optional)

1. Place corned beef in **CROCK-POT**® slow cooker. Add sauerkraut, broth, onion, garlic, peppercorns and caraway seeds. Cover; cook on LOW 7 to 9 hours.

2. Remove corned beef to large cutting board. Let stand 10 minutes. Cut across grain into 16 slices. Cut each slice into 3 pieces. Place 2 pieces corned beef on each of 24 slices of bread. Place 1 heaping tablespoon sauerkraut on each sandwich. Cut each slice of Swiss cheese into quarters; place 2 quarters on each sandwich. Spread remaining 24 slices of bread with mustard, if desired, and place on top of sandwiches.

BACON-WRAPPED DATES

MAKES 8 TO 10 SERVINGS

4 ounces goat cheese or blue cheese

1 package (8 ounces) dried pitted dates

1 pound thick-cut bacon (about 11 slices), halved

1. Fill **CROCK-POT®** slow cooker with about ½ inch of water. Spoon goat cheese evenly into centers of dates; close. Wrap half slice of bacon around each date; secure with toothpicks.

2. Heat large skillet over medium heat. Add wrapped dates; cook and turn 5 to 10 minutes until browned. Remove to **CROCK-POT®** slow cooker.

3. Cover; cook on LOW 2 to 3 hours. Remove toothpicks before serving.

SOUPS, STEWS AND CHILIES

EASY CORN CHOWDER

MAKES 6 SERVINGS

2 cans (about 14 ounces *each*) chicken broth

1 bag (16 ounces) frozen corn, thawed

3 small red potatoes, cut into ½-inch pieces

1 red bell pepper, diced

1 medium onion, diced

1 stalk celery, sliced

½ teaspoon salt

½ teaspoon black pepper

¼ teaspoon ground coriander

½ cup whipping cream

8 slices bacon, crisp-cooked and crumbled

1. Place broth, corn, potatoes, bell pepper, onion, celery, salt, black pepper and coriander in **CROCK-POT®** slow cooker. Cover; cook on LOW 7 to 8 hours.

2. Partially mash soup mixture with potato masher to thicken. Turn **CROCK-POT®** slow cooker to HIGH. Stir in cream. Cook, uncovered, on HIGH 10 minutes until heated through. Sprinkle each serving evenly with bacon.

NORTHWEST BEEF AND VEGETABLE SOUP

MAKES 6 TO 8 SERVINGS

2 tablespoons olive oil

1 pound cubed beef stew meat

1 onion, chopped

1 clove garlic, minced

8 cups water

3½ cups canned crushed tomatoes, undrained

1 butternut squash, cut into 1-inch pieces

1 can (about 15 ounces) white beans, rinsed and drained

1 turnip, peeled and cut into 1-inch pieces

1 large potato, cut into 1-inch pieces

2 stalks celery, sliced

2 tablespoons minced fresh basil

1½ teaspoons salt

1 teaspoon black pepper

1. Heat oil in large skillet over medium heat. Add beef; cook and stir 6 to 8 minutes or until browned on all sides. Add onion and garlic during last few minutes of browning. Remove to **CROCK-POT**® slow cooker.

2. Add water, tomatoes, squash, beans, turnip, potato, celery, basil, salt and pepper; stir to blend. Cover; cook on HIGH 2 hours. Turn **CROCK-POT**® slow cooker to LOW. Cover; cook on LOW 4 to 6 hours.

CORN CHIP CHILI

MAKES 6 SERVINGS

1 tablespoon olive oil

1 medium onion, chopped

1 medium red bell pepper, chopped

1 jalapeño pepper, seeded and finely chopped*

4 cloves garlic, minced

2 pounds ground beef

1 can (4 ounces) diced mild green chiles, drained

2 cans (about 14 ounces *each*) fire-roasted diced tomatoes

2 tablespoons chili powder

1½ teaspoons ground cumin

1½ teaspoons dried oregano

¾ teaspoon salt

3 cups corn chips

1 cup (4 ounces) shredded sharp Cheddar cheese

6 tablespoons chopped green onions

*Jalapeño peppers can sting and irritate the skin, so wear rubber gloves when handling peppers and do not touch your eyes.

1. Coat inside of **CROCK-POT®** slow cooker with nonstick cooking spray.

2. Heat oil in large skillet over medium-high heat. Add onion, bell pepper, jalapeño pepper and garlic; cook and stir 2 minutes or until softened. Add beef; cook and stir 10 to 12 minutes or until beef is no longer pink and liquid has evaporated. Stir in green chiles; cook 1 minute. Remove beef mixture to **CROCK-POT®** slow cooker using slotted spoon. Stir in tomatoes, chili powder, cumin and oregano.

3. Cover; cook on LOW 6 to 7 hours or on HIGH 3 to 4 hours. Stir in salt. Place corn chips evenly into serving bowls; top with chili. Sprinkle evenly with cheese and green onions.

NEW ENGLAND CLAM CHOWDER

MAKES 6 TO 8 SERVINGS

6 slices bacon, diced

2 medium onions, chopped

5 cans (6½ ounces *each*) clams, drained and liquid reserved

6 medium red potatoes, cubed

2 tablespoons minced garlic

1 teaspoon black pepper

2 cans (12 ounces *each*) evaporated milk

Snipped fresh chives (optional)

1. Heat large skillet over medium heat. Add bacon and onions; cook and stir 5 to 7 minutes or until crisp. Remove to **CROCK-POT®** slow cooker using slotted spoon.

2. Add enough water to reserved clam liquid to make 3 cups; pour into **CROCK-POT®** slow cooker. Add potatoes, garlic and pepper. Cover; cook on LOW 4 to 8 hours or HIGH 2 to 4 hours.

3. Stir in clams and evaporated milk. Cover; cook on LOW 30 to 45 minutes. Garnish with chives.

⭐ TIP: Chowder is a type of milk- or cream-based soup closely associated with New England. It is most often made with clams, but lobster and cod are other favored seafood ingredients. Regional variations also exist, using chicken, corn or vegetables, but a thick, creamy soup of clams, potatoes and onions is the most common.

CREAMY FARMHOUSE CHICKEN AND GARDEN SOUP

MAKES 4 SERVINGS

½ package (16 ounces) frozen pepper stir-fry vegetable mix

1 cup frozen corn

1 medium zucchini, sliced

2 bone-in chicken thighs, skinned

½ teaspoon minced garlic

1 can (about 14 ounces) chicken broth

½ teaspoon dried thyme

2 ounces uncooked egg noodles

1 cup half-and-half

½ cup frozen peas, thawed

2 tablespoons finely chopped fresh Italian parsley

2 tablespoons butter

1 teaspoon salt

½ teaspoon black pepper

1. Coat inside of **CROCK-POT®** slow cooker with nonstick cooking spray. Place stir-fry vegetables, corn and zucchini in bottom. Add chicken, garlic, broth and thyme. Cover; cook on HIGH 3 to 4 hours or until chicken is no longer pink in center. Remove chicken; set aside to cool slightly.

2. Add noodles to **CROCK-POT®** slow cooker. Cover; cook on HIGH 20 minutes or until noodles are heated through.

3. Meanwhile, debone and chop chicken. Return to **CROCK-POT®** slow cooker. Stir in half-and-half, peas, parsley, butter, salt and pepper. Turn off heat. Let stand, covered, 5 minutes before serving.

SOUTHWEST CHIPOTLE CHILI

MAKES 12 SERVINGS

3 links chorizo sausage (1 pound *total*), casings removed

1 pound ground beef

3 cans (about 14 ounces *each*) diced tomatoes

1 can (about 15 ounces) dark red kidney beans, rinsed and drained

1 can (about 15 ounces) black beans, rinsed and drained

1 can (about 14 ounces) stewed tomatoes, plus 1 can water

1 can (about 14 ounces) tomato sauce

2 medium green bell peppers, chopped

3 canned chipotle peppers in adobo sauce, chopped, plus 1 tablespoon adobo sauce reserved*

2 to 3 small serrano peppers, chopped*

1 poblano pepper, chopped*

1 medium onion, chopped

2 tablespoons ground red pepper

2 tablespoons chili powder

2 tablespoons hot pepper sauce

1 tablespoon sugar

Salt and black pepper

Chipotle, serrano and poblano peppers can sting and irritate the skin. Wear rubber gloves when handling peppers and do not touch your eyes.

1. Brown chorizo and ground beef in large skillet over medium-high heat 6 to 8 minutes, stirring to break up meat. Drain fat.

2. Combine chorizo and beef, diced tomatoes, beans, stewed tomatoes with water, tomato sauce, bell peppers, chipotle peppers with reserved sauce, serrano peppers, poblano pepper, onion, ground red pepper, chili powder, hot pepper sauce, sugar, salt and black pepper in **CROCK-POT**® slow cooker. Cover; cook on LOW 5 to 6 hours or on HIGH 2 to 3 hours.

SUPER-EASY CHICKEN NOODLE SOUP

MAKES 4 SERVINGS

1 can (about 48 ounces) chicken broth

2 boneless, skinless chicken breasts, cut into 1-inch pieces

4 cups water

⅔ cup diced onion

⅔ cup diced celery

⅔ cup diced carrots

⅔ cup sliced mushrooms

½ cup frozen peas

4 cubes chicken bouillon

2 tablespoons butter

1 tablespoon chopped Italian parsley

1 teaspoon salt

1 teaspoon ground cumin

1 teaspoon dried marjoram

1 teaspoon black pepper

2 cups cooked egg noodles

French bread (optional)

Combine broth, chicken, water, onion, celery, carrots, mushrooms, peas, bouillon, butter, parsley, salt, cumin, marjoram and pepper in **CROCK-POT®** slow cooker. Cover; cook on LOW 5 to 7 hours or on HIGH 3 to 4 hours. Stir in noodles during last 30 minutes of cooking. Serve with bread, if desired.

CAPE COD STEW

MAKES 8 SERVINGS

2 pounds medium raw shrimp, peeled and deveined

2 pounds fresh cod or other white fish

3 lobsters (1½ to 2½ pounds *each*), uncooked

1 pound mussels or clams, scrubbed

2 cans (about 14 ounces *each*) chopped tomatoes

4 cups beef broth

½ cup chopped onion

½ cup chopped carrot

½ cup chopped fresh cilantro

2 tablespoons sea salt

2 teaspoons crushed or minced garlic

2 teaspoons lemon juice

4 whole bay leaves

1 teaspoon dried thyme

½ teaspoon saffron threads

1. Cut shrimp and fish into bite-size pieces and place in large bowl; refrigerate. Remove lobster tails and claws. Chop tail into 2-inch pieces and separate claws at joints. Place lobster and mussels in large bowl; refrigerate.

2. Combine tomatoes, broth, onion, carrot, cilantro, salt, garlic, lemon juice, bay leaves, thyme and saffron in **CROCK-POT**® slow cooker; stir to blend. Cover; cook on LOW 7 hours.

3. Add seafood. Turn **CROCK-POT**® slow cooker to HIGH. Cover; cook on HIGH 45 minutes to 1 hour or until seafood is just cooked through. Remove and discard bay leaves. Discard any mussels that do not open.

BROCCOLI CHEDDAR SOUP

MAKES 6 SERVINGS

3 tablespoons butter

1 medium onion, chopped

3 tablespoons all-purpose flour

¼ teaspoon ground nutmeg

¼ teaspoon black pepper

4 cups vegetable broth

1 large bunch broccoli, chopped

1 medium red potato, peeled and chopped

1 teaspoon salt

1 whole bay leaf

1½ cups (6 ounces) shredded Cheddar cheese, plus additional for garnish

½ cup whipping cream

1. Melt butter in medium saucepan over medium heat. Add onion; cook and stir 6 minutes or until softened. Add flour, nutmeg and pepper; cook and stir 1 minute. Remove to **CROCK-POT**® slow cooker. Stir in broth, broccoli, potato, salt and bay leaf.

2. Cover; cook on HIGH 3 hours. Remove and discard bay leaf. Add soup in batches to food processor or blender; purée until desired consistency. Pour soup back into **CROCK-POT**® slow cooker. Stir in 1½ cups cheese and cream until cheese is melted. Garnish with additional cheese.

⭐ TIP: Though grown in Italy for centuries, broccoli didn't become popular in the United States until the 1920's when it began appearing in the home gardens of Italian immigrants. This vegetable, a member of the cabbage family, has a thick, rigid green stalk topped with deep green or purple-green heads. The heads are made up of hundreds of buds, which if left to bloom, would open into yellow flowers. The majority of broccoli in the United States is grown in the Salinas Valley of California.

WHITE CHICKEN CHILI

MAKES 6 TO 8 SERVINGS

8 ounces dried navy beans, rinsed and sorted

1 tablespoon vegetable oil

2 pounds boneless, skinless chicken breasts (about 4)

2 onions, chopped

1 tablespoon minced garlic

2 teaspoons ground cumin

2 teaspoons salt

1 teaspoon dried oregano

¼ teaspoon black pepper

¼ teaspoon ground red pepper (optional)

4 cups chicken broth

1 can (4 ounces) fire-roasted diced mild green chiles, rinsed and drained

¼ cup chopped fresh cilantro

1. Place beans in bottom of **CROCK-POT**® slow cooker. Heat oil in large skillet over medium-high heat. Add chicken; cook 8 minutes or until browned on all sides. Remove to **CROCK-POT**® slow cooker.

2. Heat same skillet over medium heat. Add onions; cook 6 minutes or until softened and lightly browned. Add garlic, cumin, salt, oregano, black pepper and ground red pepper, if desired; cook and stir 1 minute. Add broth and chiles; bring to a simmer, stirring to scrape up any browned bits from bottom of skillet. Remove onion mixture to **CROCK-POT**® slow cooker.

3. Cover; cook on LOW 5 hours. Remove chicken to large cutting board; shred with two forks. Return chicken to **CROCK-POT**® slow cooker. Top each serving with cilantro.

EASY BEEF STEW

MAKES 6 TO 8 SERVINGS

1½ to 2 pounds cubed beef stew meat

4 medium potatoes, cubed

4 carrots, cut into 1½-inch pieces *or* 4 cups baby carrots

1 medium onion, cut into 8 slices

2 cans (8 ounces *each*) tomato sauce

1 teaspoon salt

½ teaspoon black pepper

Combine beef, potatoes, carrots, onion, tomato sauce, salt and pepper in **CROCK-POT**® slow cooker; stir to blend. Cover; cook on LOW 8 to 10 hours.

PIZZA SOUP

MAKES 4 SERVINGS

2 cans (about 14 ounces *each*) stewed tomatoes with Italian seasonings, undrained

2 cups beef broth

1 cup sliced mushrooms

1 small onion, chopped

1 tablespoon tomato paste

¼ teaspoon salt

¼ teaspoon black pepper

½ pound turkey Italian sausage, casings removed

Shredded mozzarella cheese

1. Combine tomatoes, broth, mushrooms, onion, tomato paste, salt and pepper in **CROCK-POT**® slow cooker; stir to blend.

2. Shape sausage into marble-size balls; stir into soup mixture. Cover; cook on LOW 6 to 7 hours. Top with cheese.

COD FISH STEW

MAKES 6 TO 8 SERVINGS

½ pound bacon, coarsely chopped

1 large carrot, diced

1 large onion, diced

2 stalks celery, diced

2 cloves garlic, minced

Salt and black pepper

3 cups water

2 cups clam juice or fish broth

1 can (28 ounces) plum tomatoes, drained

2 potatoes, diced

½ cup dry white wine

3 tablespoons chopped fresh Italian parsley

3 tablespoons tomato paste

3 saffron threads

2½ pounds fresh cod, skinned and cut into 2-inch pieces

1. Heat medium skillet over medium heat. Add bacon; cook and stir until crisp. Add carrot, onion, celery, garlic, salt and pepper; cook and stir 6 to 8 minutes until vegetables soften.

2. Remove bacon and vegetables to **CROCK-POT**® slow cooker using slotted spoon. Stir in water, clam juice, tomatoes, potatoes, wine, parsley, tomato paste and saffron. Cover; cook on LOW 6 to 7 hours or on HIGH 3 to 4 hours.

3. Add cod. Cover; cook on HIGH 10 to 20 minutes or until cod is just cooked through.

CAULIFLOWER SOUP

MAKES 8 SERVINGS

2 heads cauliflower, cut into small florets

8 cups chicken broth

¾ cup chopped celery

¾ cup chopped onion

2 teaspoons salt

2 teaspoons black pepper

2 cups milk or light cream

1 teaspoon Worcestershire sauce

1. Combine cauliflower, broth, celery, onion, salt and pepper in **CROCK-POT®** slow cooker. Cover; cook on LOW 7 to 8 hours or on HIGH 3 to 4 hours.

2. Pour cauliflower mixture into food processor or blender; process until smooth. Add milk and Worcestershire sauce; process until blended. Pour soup back into **CROCK-POT®** slow cooker. Cover; cook on HIGH 15 to 20 minutes or until heated through.

PLANTATION PEANUT SOUP

MAKES 8 SERVINGS

6 cups chicken broth

2 cups whipping cream

1 cup chunky peanut butter

1 cup chopped peanuts, divided

½ cup chopped onion

½ cup chopped celery

4 tablespoons (½ stick) butter

½ teaspoon salt

½ cup water

½ cup all-purpose flour

1. Combine broth, cream, peanut butter, ½ cup peanuts, onion, celery, butter and salt in **CROCK-POT®** slow cooker. Cover; cook on LOW 4 hours.

2. Turn **CROCK-POT®** slow cooker to HIGH. Stir water into flour in small bowl until smooth; whisk into soup. Cover; cook on HIGH 20 to 25 minutes or until thickened, stirring occasionally. Garnish each serving with remaining ½ cup peanuts.

Cauliflower Soup

MANHATTAN CLAM CHOWDER

MAKES 4 SERVINGS

3 slices bacon, diced

2 stalks celery, chopped

3 onions, chopped

2 cups water

1 can (about 14 ounces) stewed tomatoes, undrained and chopped

4 small red potatoes, diced

2 carrots, diced

½ teaspoon dried thyme

½ teaspoon black pepper

½ teaspoon hot pepper sauce

1 pound minced fresh clams*

*You may substitute 6 cans (6½ ounces each) clams, which yield about 1 pound. Drain and discard liquid.

1. Heat large skillet over medium heat. Add bacon; cook and stir until crisp. Remove to **CROCK-POT**® slow cooker using slotted spoon.

2. Add celery and onions to skillet; cook and stir 6 to 8 minutes or until tender. Remove to **CROCK-POT**® slow cooker using slotted spoon.

3. Stir in water, tomatoes, potatoes, carrots, thyme, black pepper and hot pepper sauce. Cover; cook on LOW 6 to 8 hours or on HIGH 3 to 4 hours. Add clams during last half hour of cooking.

CLASSIC CHILI

MAKES 6 SERVINGS

1½ pounds ground beef

1½ cups chopped onion

1 cup chopped green bell pepper

2 cloves garlic, minced

3 cans (about 15 ounces *each*) dark red kidney beans, rinsed and drained

2 cans (about 15 ounces *each*) tomato sauce

1 can (about 14 ounces) diced tomatoes

2 to 3 teaspoons chili powder

1 to 2 teaspoons ground mustard

¾ teaspoon dried basil

½ teaspoon black pepper

1 to 2 dried red chiles (optional)

Shredded Cheddar cheese (optional)

Sprigs fresh cilantro (optional)

1. Brown beef, onion, bell pepper and garlic in large skillet over medium-high heat 6 to 8 minutes, stirring to break up meat. Remove beef mixture to **CROCK-POT**® slow cooker using slotted spoon.

2. Add beans, tomato sauce, tomatoes, chili powder, mustard, basil, black pepper and chiles, if desired, to **CROCK-POT**® slow cooker; stir to blend. Cover; cook on LOW 8 to 10 hours or on HIGH 4 to 5 hours. If used, remove chiles before serving. Top with cheese, if desired. Garnish with cilantro.

A SALUTE TO DINNER

HARVEST HAM SUPPER

MAKES 6 SERVINGS

6 carrots, cut into 2-inch pieces

3 medium unpeeled sweet potatoes, quartered

1 to 1½ pounds boneless ham

1 cup maple syrup

Chopped fresh Italian parsley (optional)

Arrange carrots and potatoes in bottom of **CROCK-POT**® slow cooker. Place ham on top of vegetables. Pour maple syrup over ham and vegetables. Cover; cook on LOW 6 to 8 hours. Garnish vegetables with parsley.

HOT BEEF SANDWICHES AU JUS

MAKES 8 TO 10 SERVINGS

4 pounds boneless beef bottom round roast, trimmed*

2 cans (about 10 ounces *each*) condensed beef broth, undiluted

1 can (12 ounces) beer

2 envelopes (1 ounce *each*) onion soup mix

1 tablespoon minced garlic

2 teaspoons sugar

1 teaspoon dried oregano

Crusty French rolls, sliced in half

Unless you have a 5-, 6- or 7-quart CROCK-POT® slow cooker, cut any roast larger than 2½ pounds in half so it cooks completely.

1. Place beef in **CROCK-POT®** slow cooker. Combine broth, beer, dry soup mix, garlic, sugar and oregano in large bowl; stir to blend. Pour mixture over beef. Cover; cook on HIGH 6 to 8 hours.

2. Remove beef to large cutting board; shred with two forks. Return beef to cooking liquid; stir to blend. Serve on rolls with cooking liquid for dipping.

BARBECUE RIBS

MAKES 6 SERVINGS

Olive oil

2 small red onions, finely chopped

3 to 4 cloves garlic, minced

1 cup packed brown sugar

1 cup ketchup

½ cup cider vinegar

Juice of 1 lemon

2 tablespoons Worcestershire sauce

1 tablespoon hot pepper sauce

½ teaspoon chili powder

2 racks pork baby back ribs, cut into 3- to 4-rib sections

1. Heat oil in large skillet over medium heat. Add onions and garlic; cook and stir 3 to 5 minutes or until softened. Stir in brown sugar, ketchup, vinegar, lemon juice, Worcestershire sauce, hot pepper sauce and chili powder; cook and stir 5 minutes. Remove half of sauce to **CROCK-POT**® slow cooker. Reserve remaining sauce in skillet.

2. Add ribs to **CROCK-POT**® slow cooker; turn to coat. Cover; cook on LOW 7 to 9 hours or on HIGH 4 to 6 hours. Serve ribs with reserved sauce.

⭐ **TIP:** More juice will be available from a lemon if it is at room temperature. If time is short, warm a cold lemon in the microwave oven at HIGH power for about 30 seconds. Roll them around on the counter under the flat of your hand before cutting them in half. This releases juice from the small sacs of the lemon. A reamer or juicer, either hand or electric, can be used to extract juice.

TUNA CASSEROLE

MAKES 6 SERVINGS

2 cans (10¾ ounces *each*) cream of celery soup

2 cans (5 ounces *each*) tuna in water, drained and flaked

1 cup water

2 carrots, chopped

1 small red onion, chopped

¼ teaspoon black pepper

1 raw egg, uncracked

8 ounces hot cooked egg noodles

Plain dry bread crumbs

2 tablespoons chopped fresh Italian parsley

1. Stir soup, tuna, water, carrots, onion and pepper into **CROCK-POT®** slow cooker. Place whole unpeeled egg on top. Cover; cook on LOW 4 to 5 hours or on HIGH 1½ to 3 hours.

2. Remove egg; stir in pasta. Cover; cook on HIGH 30 to 60 minutes or until pasta is tender. Meanwhile, peel egg and mash in small bowl; mix in bread crumbs and parsley. Top casserole with bread crumb mixture.

CLASSIC POT ROAST

MAKES 6 TO 8 SERVINGS

1 tablespoon vegetable oil

1 boneless beef chuck shoulder roast (3 to 4 pounds)*

6 medium potatoes, cut into halves

6 carrots, sliced

2 medium onions, cut into quarters

2 stalks celery, sliced

1 can (about 14 ounces) diced tomatoes

Salt and black pepper

Dried oregano

2 tablespoons water

1½ to 2 tablespoons all-purpose flour

*Unless you have a 5-, 6- or 7-quart **CROCK-POT**® slow cooker, cut any roast larger than 2½ pounds in half so it cooks completely.

1. Heat oil in large skillet over medium-low heat. Add roast; cook 6 to 8 minutes or until browned on all sides. Remove to **CROCK-POT**® slow cooker.

2. Add potatoes, carrots, onions, celery, tomatoes, salt, pepper, oregano and enough water to cover bottom of **CROCK-POT**® slow cooker by about ½ inch. Cover; cook on LOW 8 to 10 hours.

3. Turn off heat. Remove roast and vegetables to large serving platter using slotted spoon. Let cooking liquid stand 5 minutes. Skim off fat and discard. Turn **CROCK-POT**® slow cooker to HIGH. Stir 2 tablespoons water into flour in small bowl until smooth; whisk into cooking liquid. Cover; cook on HIGH 10 to 15 minutes or until thickened. Serve sauce over roast and vegetables.

MAPLE-DRY RUBBED RIBS

MAKES 4 SERVINGS

2 teaspoons chili powder, divided

1 teaspoon ground coriander

1 teaspoon garlic powder, divided

½ teaspoon salt

¼ teaspoon black pepper

3 to 3½ pounds pork baby back ribs, trimmed and cut in half

3 tablespoons maple syrup, divided

1 can (about 8 ounces) tomato sauce

¼ teaspoon ground cinnamon

¼ teaspoon ground ginger

1. Coat inside of **CROCK-POT**® slow cooker with nonstick cooking spray. Combine 1 teaspoon chili powder, coriander, ½ teaspoon garlic powder, salt and pepper in small bowl; stir to blend. Brush ribs with 1 tablespoon maple syrup; sprinkle with spice mixture. Remove ribs to **CROCK-POT**® slow cooker.

2. Combine tomato sauce, remaining 1 teaspoon chili powder, ½ teaspoon garlic powder, 2 tablespoons maple syrup, cinnamon and ginger in medium bowl; stir to blend. Pour tomato sauce mixture over ribs in **CROCK-POT**® slow cooker. Cover; cook on LOW 8 to 9 hours.

3. Remove ribs to large serving platter; cover with foil to keep warm. Turn **CROCK-POT**® slow cooker to HIGH. Cover; cook on HIGH 10 to 15 minutes or until sauce is thickened. Brush ribs with sauce and serve any remaining sauce on the side.

CAMPFIRED-UP SLOPPY JOES

MAKES 6 SERVINGS

1½ pounds ground beef

½ cup chopped sweet onion

1 medium red bell pepper, chopped

1 large clove garlic, crushed

½ cup ketchup

½ cup barbecue sauce

2 tablespoons cider vinegar

1 tablespoon Worcestershire sauce

1 tablespoon packed brown sugar

1 teaspoon chili powder

1 can (about 8 ounces) baked beans

6 Kaiser rolls, split and warmed

Shredded sharp Cheddar cheese (optional)

1. Brown ground beef, onion, bell pepper and garlic in large skillet over medium-high heat 6 to 8 minutes, stirring to break up meat. Remove beef mixture to **CROCK-POT**® slow cooker using slotted spoon.

2. Combine ketchup, barbecue sauce, vinegar, Worcestershire sauce, brown sugar and chili powder in small bowl. Remove to **CROCK-POT**® slow cooker. Stir in beans. Cover; cook on HIGH 3 hours.

3. To serve, spoon meat mixture evenly onto roll bottoms. Sprinkle with Cheddar cheese, if desired, before topping sandwiches with roll tops.

HEAVENLY HARVEST PORK ROAST

MAKES 10 SERVINGS

¼ cup pomegranate juice

¼ cup sugar

1 tablespoon salt

1 tablespoon garlic salt

1 tablespoon steak seasoning

1 teaspoon black pepper

1 lean pork loin roast
   (2¾ pounds)*

2 pears, cored, peeled and
   sliced thick

2 oranges with peel, sliced
   thick

*Unless you have a 5-, 6- or 7-quart
CROCK-POT® slow cooker, cut any roast
larger than 2½ pounds in half so it cooks
completely.*

1. Combine pomegranate juice and sugar in small saucepan; cook and stir about 2 minutes or until sugar dissolves. Pour into **CROCK-POT**® slow cooker.

2. Blend salt, garlic salt, steak seasoning and pepper in small bowl. Rub mixture over roast. Place roast in **CROCK-POT**® slow cooker. Turn roast to cover with juice mixture.

3. Top roast with pear and orange slices. Cover; cook on HIGH 6 to 8 hours or until tender. Serve with juice and fruit slices.

EASY SALISBURY STEAK

MAKES 4 SERVINGS

1 medium onion, sliced

1½ pounds ground beef

1 egg

½ cup seasoned dry bread crumbs

2 teaspoons Worcestershire sauce, divided

1 teaspoon dry mustard

1 can (10½ ounces) cream of mushroom soup

½ cup water

3 tablespoons ketchup

½ cup sliced mushrooms

Chopped fresh Italian parsley (optional)

Mashed potatoes (optional)

Steamed peas (optional)

1. Coat inside of **CROCK-POT**® slow cooker with nonstick cooking spray. Layer onion on bottom of **CROCK-POT**® slow cooker.

2. Combine beef, egg, bread crumbs, 1 teaspoon Worcestershire sauce and dry mustard in large bowl. Form into four 1-inch-thick oval patties. Heat large nonstick skillet over medium-high heat. Add patties; cook 2 minutes per side or until lightly browned. Remove to **CROCK-POT**® slow cooker. Stir soup, water, ketchup and remaining 1 teaspoon Worcestershire sauce in medium bowl. Pour mixture over patties; top with mushrooms. Cover; cook on LOW 3 to 3½ hours. Garnish with parsley. Serve with potatoes and peas, if desired.

PULLED PORK WITH COLA BARBECUE SAUCE

MAKES 8 SERVINGS

1 teaspoon vegetable oil

3 pounds boneless pork shoulder roast, cut into 4 equal pieces

1 cup cola

¼ cup tomato paste

2 tablespoons packed brown sugar

2 teaspoons Worcestershire sauce

2 teaspoons spicy brown mustard

Hot pepper sauce

Salt

8 hamburger buns

1. Heat oil in large skillet over medium-high heat. Add pork; cook 5 to 7 minutes until browned on all sides. Remove to **CROCK-POT**® slow cooker. Pour cola over pork. Cover; cook on LOW 7½ to 8 hours or on HIGH 3½ to 4 hours.

2. Turn off heat. Remove pork to large plate; cover with foil. Let cooking liquid stand 5 minutes. Skim off and discard fat. Turn **CROCK-POT**® slow cooker to HIGH. Whisk in tomato paste, brown sugar, Worcestershire sauce and mustard. Cover; cook on HIGH 15 minutes or until thickened.

3. Shred pork with two forks. Stir pork back into **CROCK-POT**® slow cooker. Season with hot pepper sauce and salt. Serve on buns.

CHILI AND CHEESE "BAKED" POTATO SUPPER

MAKES 4 SERVINGS

4 russet potatoes (about 2 pounds), unpeeled

2 cups prepared chili

½ cup (2 ounces) shredded Cheddar cheese

2 green onions, sliced

¼ cup sour cream (optional)

1. Prick potatoes in several places with fork. Wrap potatoes in foil. Place in **CROCK-POT®** slow cooker. Cover; cook on LOW 8 to 10 hours or on HIGH 4 to 5 hours.

2. Carefully unwrap potatoes and place on serving dish. Place chili in medium microwavable dish; microwave on HIGH 3 to 5 minutes. Split potatoes and spoon chili on top. Top with cheese, green onions and sour cream, if desired.

HAM AND POTATO HASH

MAKES 6 TO 7 SERVINGS

1½ pounds red potatoes, sliced

8 ounces thinly sliced ham

2 poblano peppers, cut into thin strips

2 tablespoons olive oil

1 tablespoon dried oregano

¼ teaspoon salt

1 cup (4 ounces) shredded Monterey Jack or pepper jack cheese

2 tablespoons finely chopped fresh cilantro

1. Combine potatoes, ham, poblano peppers, oil and oregano in **CROCK-POT®** slow cooker; stir to blend. Cover; cook on LOW 7 hours or on HIGH 4 hours.

2. Remove mixture to large serving platter; sprinkle with cheese and cilantro. Let stand 3 minutes or until cheese is melted.

Chili and Cheese
"Baked" Potato Supper

PEPPERONI PIZZA MONKEY BREAD

MAKES 12 SERVINGS

1 package (about 3 ounces) pepperoni, divided

1 teaspoon minced garlic

¼ teaspoon red pepper flakes

1 package (about 16 ounces) refrigerated biscuits, each biscuit cut into 6 pieces

1 can (15 ounces) pizza sauce

1 small green bell pepper, chopped

1 small yellow bell pepper, chopped

1 package (8 ounces) shredded mozzarella cheese

1. Coat inside of **CROCK-POT**® slow cooker with nonstick cooking spray. Prepare foil handles by tearing off four 18×2-inch strips heavy foil (or use regular foil folded to double thickness). Crisscross foil strips in spoke design; place in round **CROCK-POT**® slow cooker. Spray foil handles with cooking spray.

2. Chop half of pepperoni slices. Combine chopped pepperoni, garlic and red pepper flakes in medium bowl. Roll each biscuit piece into pepperoni mixture; place in **CROCK-POT**® slow cooker. Pour half of pizza sauce over dough. Reserve remaining pizza sauce. Top sauce with bell peppers, cheese and remaining half of pepperoni slices.

3. Cover; cook on LOW 3 hours. Turn off heat. Let pizza stand 10 to 15 minutes. Remove from **CROCK-POT**® slow cooker using foil handles. Serve with remaining pizza sauce for dipping.

CAJUN POT ROAST

MAKES 6 SERVINGS

- 1 boneless beef chuck roast (3 pounds)*
- 1 to 2 tablespoons Cajun seasoning
- 1 tablespoon vegetable oil
- 1 can (about 14 ounces) diced tomatoes
- 1 can (about 14 ounces) diced tomatoes with mild green chiles
- 1 medium onion, chopped
- 1 cup chopped rutabaga
- 1 cup chopped mushrooms
- 1 cup chopped turnip
- 1 cup chopped parsnip
- 1 cup chopped green bell pepper
- 1 cup green beans
- 1 cup sliced carrots
- 1 cup corn
- 2 tablespoons hot pepper sauce
- 1 teaspoon sugar
- ½ teaspoon black pepper
- ¾ cup water

*Unless you have a 5-, 6- or 7-quart CROCK-POT® slow cooker, cut any roast larger than 2½ pounds in half so it cooks completely.

1. Coat inside of **CROCK-POT**® slow cooker with nonstick cooking spray. Season roast with Cajun seasoning. Heat oil in large skillet over medium-high heat. Add roast; cook 5 minutes on each side until browned.

2. Place roast, tomatoes, onion, rutabaga, mushrooms, turnip, parsnip, bell pepper, green beans, carrots, corn, hot pepper sauce, sugar and black pepper in **CROCK-POT**® slow cooker. Pour in water. Cover; cook on LOW 6 hours.

CHEESY SHRIMP ON GRITS

MAKES 6 SERVINGS

1 cup finely chopped green bell pepper

1 cup finely chopped red bell pepper

½ cup thinly sliced celery

1 bunch green onions, chopped and divided

¼ cup (½ stick) butter, cubed

1¼ teaspoons seafood seasoning

2 whole bay leaves

¼ teaspoon ground red pepper

1 pound medium raw shrimp, peeled and deveined

5⅓ cups water

1⅓ cups quick-cooking grits

2 cups (8 ounces) shredded sharp Cheddar cheese

¼ cup whipping cream or half-and-half

1. Coat inside of **CROCK-POT**® slow cooker with nonstick cooking spray. Add bell peppers, celery, all but ½ cup green onions, butter, seafood seasoning, bay leaves and ground red pepper. Cover; cook on LOW 4 hours or on HIGH 2 hours.

2. Add shrimp. Cover; cook on HIGH 15 minutes.

3. Meanwhile, bring water to a boil in medium saucepan. Add grits; cook according to package directions.

4. Remove and discard bay leaves. Stir in cheese, cream and remaining ½ cup green onions. Cook, uncovered, on HIGH 5 minutes or until cheese is melted. Serve over grits.

CHEESEBURGER POTATO CASSEROLE

MAKES 6 SERVINGS

1 pound ground beef

½ cup chopped onion

1 can (about 10¾ ounces) Cheddar cheese soup

¼ cup sweet pickle relish

2 tablespoons brown mustard

2 tablespoons ketchup, plus additional for topping

1 tablespoon Worcestershire sauce

1 package (30 ounces) shredded potatoes

2 cups (8 ounces) shredded Cheddar cheese

1 teaspoon salt

½ teaspoon black pepper

Green onions (optional)

1. Coat inside of **CROCK-POT®** slow cooker with nonstick cooking spray. Brown beef and onion in large skillet over medium-high heat 6 to 8 minutes, stirring to break up meat. Stir in cheese soup, relish, mustard, 2 tablespoons ketchup and Worcestershire sauce until well blended.

2. Arrange half of potatoes in bottom of **CROCK-POT®** slow cooker. Spoon half of meat mixture over potatoes. Sprinkle with 1½ cups cheese, ½ teaspoon salt and ¼ teaspoon pepper. Add remaining meat mixture; sprinkle with remaining ½ cup cheese, ½ teaspoon salt and ¼ teaspoon pepper. Cover; cook on LOW 4 hours or on HIGH 2 hours. Top with additional ketchup and green onions, if desired.

PATRIOTIC SIDES

MACARONI AND CHEESE

MAKES 6 TO 8 SERVINGS

6 cups cooked elbow macaroni

2 tablespoons butter

6 cups (24 ounces) shredded Cheddar cheese

4 cups evaporated milk

2 teaspoons salt

½ teaspoon black pepper

Toss macaroni with butter in large bowl. Stir in cheese, evaporated milk, salt and pepper. Remove to **CROCK-POT®** slow cooker. Cover; cook on HIGH 2 to 3 hours.

★ **TIP:** As a general rule, 2 ounces of dry pasta is equal to a side-dish serving. Fresh pasta is much moister and does not expand, so use 3 ounces of fresh pasta for each side-dish serving.

WHITE BEANS AND TOMATOES

MAKES 8 TO 10 SERVINGS

¼ cup olive oil

2 medium onions, chopped

1 tablespoon minced garlic

4 cups water

2 cans (about 14 ounces *each*) cannellini beans, rinsed and drained

1 can (about 28 ounces) crushed tomatoes

4 teaspoons dried oregano

2 teaspoons kosher salt

Black pepper (optional)

Sprigs fresh oregano (optional)

1. Heat oil in large skillet over medium heat. Add onions; cook 15 minutes or until tender and translucent, stirring occasionally. Add garlic; cook 1 minute.

2. Remove mixture to **CROCK-POT**® slow cooker. Add water, beans, tomatoes, dried oregano and salt. Cover; cook on LOW 8 hours or on HIGH 4 hours. Stir in pepper, if desired. Garnish with fresh oregano.

CHEESY MASHED POTATO CASSEROLE

MAKES 10 TO 12 SERVINGS

4 pounds Yukon Gold potatoes, cut into 1-inch pieces

2 cups vegetable broth

3 tablespoons unsalted butter, cubed

½ cup milk, heated

⅓ cup sour cream

2 cups (8 ounces) shredded sharp Cheddar cheese, plus additional for garnish

½ teaspoon salt

¼ teaspoon black pepper

Chopped fresh Italian parsley (optional)

1. Coat inside of **CROCK-POT®** slow cooker with nonstick cooking spray. Add potatoes and broth; dot with butter. Cover; cook on LOW 4½ to 5 hours.

2. Mash potatoes with potato masher; stir in milk, sour cream, 2 cups cheese, salt and pepper until cheese is melted. Garnish with additional cheese and parsley.

SUPPER SQUASH MEDLEY

MAKES 8 TO 10 SERVINGS

2 butternut squash, peeled, seeded and diced

1 can (28 ounces) diced tomatoes

1 can (15 ounces) corn, drained

2 onions, chopped

2 green bell peppers, chopped

2 teaspoons minced garlic

2 mild fresh green chiles, chopped

1 cup chicken broth

1 teaspoon salt

½ teaspoon black pepper

1 can (6 ounces) tomato paste

Sprigs fresh basil (optional)

1. Combine squash, diced tomatoes, corn, onions, bell peppers, garlic, chiles, broth, salt and black pepper in **CROCK-POT**® slow cooker. Cover; cook on LOW 6 hours.

2. Remove about ½ cup cooking liquid and blend with tomato paste in small bowl. Return to **CROCK-POT**® slow cooker; stir to blend. Cover; cook on LOW 30 minutes or until mixture is slightly thickened and heated through. Garnish with basil.

TWICE "BAKED" POTATOES

MAKES 4 SERVINGS

4 baking potatoes (about 10 ounces *each*)

3 tablespoons olive oil, divided

1 head garlic

4 tablespoons sour cream

1 to 2 tablespoons milk

½ teaspoon salt

¼ teaspoon black pepper

2 slices bacon, cooked and crumbled

½ cup (2 ounces) shredded Cheddar cheese, divided

¼ teaspoon smoked paprika

Chopped green onions (optional)

1. Rub potatoes with 2 tablespoons oil; wrap each potato in foil. Place potatoes in **CROCK-POT®** slow cooker. Cut across top of garlic head. Place garlic in foil; top with remaining 1 tablespoon oil. Twist foil closed around garlic; place on top of potatoes. Cover; cook on HIGH 4 hours or until potatoes are soft when pierced with knife.

2. Pull foil away from each potato; crimp it around bottom of potatoes. Cut thin slice from top of each potato. Scoop inside of potatoes into large bowl, leaving about ¼-inch shell. Squeeze garlic head to remove softened cloves; mash with fork. Measure 1 tablespoon mashed garlic; add to large bowl with potatoes. Refrigerate remaining garlic in airtight jar for another use.

3. Add sour cream, milk, salt and pepper to large bowl with potatoes; beat with electric mixer at medium speed 3 to 4 minutes or until smooth. Stir in bacon and half of cheese. Spoon mashed potatoes into shells, mounding at top. Top with remaining cheese and paprika. Return potatoes to **CROCK-POT®** slow cooker. Cover; cook on HIGH 15 minutes or until cheese is melted. Garnish with green onions.

CHEESY BROCCOLI CASSEROLE

MAKES 4 TO 6 SERVINGS

2 packages (10 ounces *each*) frozen chopped broccoli, thawed

1 can (10½ ounces) condensed cream of celery soup, undiluted

1¼ cups (5 ounces) shredded sharp Cheddar cheese, divided

¼ cup minced onion

1 teaspoon paprika

1 teaspoon hot pepper sauce

½ teaspoon celery seed

1 cup crushed potato chips or saltine crackers

1. Coat inside of **CROCK-POT®** slow cooker with nonstick cooking spray. Combine broccoli, soup, 1 cup cheese, onion, paprika, hot pepper sauce and celery seed in **CROCK-POT®** slow cooker; stir to blend. Cover; cook on LOW 5 to 6 hours or on HIGH 2½ to 3 hours.

2. Uncover; sprinkle top with potato chips and remaining ¼ cup cheese. Cook, uncovered, on HIGH 10 to 15 minutes or until cheese is melted.

CORN ON THE COB
WITH GARLIC HERB BUTTER

MAKES 4 TO 5 SERVINGS

4 to 5 ears of corn, husked

½ cup (1 stick) unsalted butter, softened

3 to 4 cloves garlic, minced

2 tablespoons finely minced fresh Italian parsley

Salt and black pepper

1. Place each ear of corn on piece of foil. Combine butter, garlic and parsley in small bowl; spread onto corn. Season with salt and pepper; tightly seal foil.

2. Place ears in **CROCK-POT®** slow cooker, overlapping, if necessary. Add enough water to come one fourth of the way up each ear. Cover; cook on LOW 4 to 5 hours or on HIGH 2 to 2½ hours.

PARMESAN POTATO WEDGES

MAKES 6 SERVINGS

2 pounds red potatoes, cut into ½-inch wedges

¼ cup finely chopped yellow onion

1½ teaspoons dried oregano

½ teaspoon salt

¼ teaspoon black pepper

2 tablespoons butter, cubed

¼ cup grated Parmesan cheese

Layer potatoes, onion, oregano, salt and pepper in **CROCK-POT®** slow cooker; dot with butter. Cover; cook on HIGH 4 hours. Remove potatoes to large serving platter; sprinkle with cheese.

SLOW COOKER GREEN BEANS

MAKES 6 TO 8 SERVINGS

1 tablespoon olive oil

1 pound fresh green beans, trimmed and cut in half

1 teaspoon fresh garlic slivers

1 can (10½ ounces) French Onion soup

¾ cup water

¼ teaspoon black pepper

¼ cup (about 2 ounces) chopped pimientos

¼ cup sliced almonds*

*To toast almonds, spread in single layer in small heavy skillet. Cook and stir over medium heat 1 to 2 minutes or until nuts are lightly browned.

1. Heat oil in large skillet over high heat. Add beans; cook and stir 5 minutes or until beans begin to char and blister. Add garlic; cook 1 minute. Remove bean mixture to **CROCK-POT®** slow cooker.

2. Add soup, water, pepper and pimientos to **CROCK-POT®** slow cooker; stir to blend. Cover; cook on LOW 4 hours or on HIGH 2 hours. Sprinkle almonds over beans just before serving.

⭐ **TIP:** For the most flavor, choose thin, crisp green beans. Avoid ones that are thick and have a leathery look to them.

SLOW-ROASTED POTATOES

MAKES 3 TO 4 SERVINGS

16 small new red potatoes, unpeeled

3 tablespoons butter, cubed

1 teaspoon paprika

½ teaspoon salt

¼ teaspoon garlic powder

Black pepper

1 to 2 tablespoons water

Combine potatoes, butter, paprika, salt, garlic powder and pepper in **CROCK-POT®** slow cooker; stir to blend. Cover; cook on LOW 7 hours or on HIGH 4 hours. Remove potatoes to large serving bowl using slotted spoon; keep warm. Add water to cooking liquid; stir until well blended. Pour over potatoes.

BBQ BAKED BEANS

MAKES 12 SERVINGS

3 cans (about 15 ounces *each*) white beans, drained

4 slices bacon, chopped

¾ cup prepared barbecue sauce

½ cup maple syrup

1½ teaspoons ground mustard

Coat inside of **CROCK-POT®** slow cooker with nonstick cooking spray. Add beans, bacon, barbecue sauce, maple syrup and ground mustard; stir to blend. Cover; cook on LOW 4 hours, stirring halfway through cooking time.

BALSAMIC-HONEY GLAZED ROOT VEGETABLES

MAKES 6 SERVINGS

4 medium carrots, cut into ½-inch pieces

2 medium parsnips, cut into ¾-inch pieces

1½ pounds sweet potatoes, peeled and cut into 1-inch pieces

2 medium red onions, each cut through root end into 6 wedges

¼ cup honey

3 tablespoons unsalted butter, melted

1 tablespoon balsamic vinegar

1 teaspoon salt

¼ teaspoon black pepper

1. Combine carrots, parsnips, sweet potatoes, onions, honey, butter, vinegar, salt and pepper in **CROCK-POT**® slow cooker; stir to coat vegetables. Cover; cook on LOW 4 to 5 hours or until vegetables are tender.

2. Remove vegetables to large bowl using slotted spoon. Turn **CROCK-POT**® slow cooker to HIGH. Cover; cook on HIGH 15 minutes or until sauce is thickened. Return vegetables to **CROCK-POT**® slow cooker; toss to coat.

SWEET POTATO AND PECAN CASSEROLE

MAKES 6 TO 8 SERVINGS

1 can (40 ounces) sweet potatoes, drained and mashed

½ cup apple juice

⅓ cup plus 2 tablespoons butter, melted and divided

½ teaspoon salt

½ teaspoon ground cinnamon

¼ teaspoon black pepper

2 eggs, beaten

⅓ cup chopped pecans

⅓ cup packed brown sugar

2 tablespoons all-purpose flour

1. Combine potatoes, apple juice, ⅓ cup butter, salt, cinnamon and pepper in large bowl; beat in eggs. Pour mixture into **CROCK-POT®** slow cooker.

2. Combine pecans, brown sugar, flour and remaining 2 tablespoons butter in small bowl; stir to blend. Spread over sweet potatoes. Cover; cook on HIGH 3 to 4 hours.

MASHED RUTABAGAS AND POTATOES

MAKES 8 SERVINGS

2 pounds rutabagas, peeled and cut into ½-inch pieces

1 pound potatoes, peeled and cut into ½-inch pieces

½ cup milk

½ teaspoon ground nutmeg

2 tablespoons chopped fresh Italian parsley

Sprigs fresh Italian parsley (optional)

1. Place rutabagas and potatoes in **CROCK-POT®** slow cooker; add enough water to cover vegetables. Cover; cook on LOW 6 hours or on HIGH 3 hours. Remove vegetables to large bowl using slotted spoon. Discard cooking liquid.

2. Mash vegetables with potato masher. Add milk, nutmeg and chopped parsley; stir until smooth. Garnish with parsley sprigs.

BUTTERMILK CORN BREAD

MAKES 1 LOAF

1½ cups cornmeal

½ cup all-purpose flour

1 tablespoon sugar

2 teaspoons baking powder

½ teaspoon salt

1½ cups buttermilk

½ teaspoon baking soda

2 eggs

¼ cup (½ stick) butter, melted

¼ cup chopped seeded jalapeño peppers*

1 tablespoon finely chopped pimientos or roasted red pepper

*Jalapeño peppers can sting and irritate the skin, so wear rubber gloves when handling peppers and do not touch your eyes.

1. Coat inside of **CROCK-POT**® slow cooker with nonstick cooking spray.

2. Sift cornmeal, flour, sugar, baking powder and salt into large bowl. Whisk buttermilk into baking soda in medium bowl. Add eggs to buttermilk mixture; whisk lightly until blended. Stir in butter.

3. Stir buttermilk mixture, jalapeño peppers and pimientos into cornmeal mixture until just blended. *Do not overmix.* Pour into **CROCK-POT**® slow cooker. Cover; cook on HIGH 1½ to 2 hours.

GREEN BEAN CASSEROLE

MAKES 6 SERVINGS

2 packages (10 ounces *each*) frozen green beans

1 can (10¾ ounces) condensed cream of mushroom soup, undiluted

1 tablespoon chopped fresh Italian parsley

1 tablespoon chopped roasted red peppers

1 teaspoon dried sage

½ teaspoon salt

½ teaspoon black pepper

¼ teaspoon ground nutmeg

½ cup toasted slivered almonds*

To toast almonds, spread in single layer in small heavy skillet. Cook and stir over medium heat 1 to 2 minutes or until nuts are lightly browned.

Combine beans, soup, parsley, red peppers, sage, salt, black pepper and nutmeg in **CROCK-POT®** slow cooker; stir to blend. Cover; cook on LOW 3 to 4 hours. Sprinkle with almonds.

CHUNKY RANCH POTATOES

MAKES 8 SERVINGS

3 pounds unpeeled red potatoes, quartered

1 cup water

½ cup prepared ranch dressing

½ cup grated Parmesan or Cheddar cheese

¼ cup minced fresh chives

1. Place potatoes in **CROCK-POT®** slow cooker. Add water. Cover; cook on LOW 7 to 9 hours or on HIGH 4 to 6 hours.

2. Stir in ranch dressing, cheese and chives. Break up potatoes into large pieces.

FIVE-INGREDIENT MUSHROOM STUFFING

MAKES 12 SERVINGS

6 tablespoons unsalted butter

2 medium onions, chopped

1 pound sliced white mushrooms

¼ teaspoon salt

5 cups bagged stuffing mix, any flavor

1 cup vegetable broth

Chopped fresh Italian parsley (optional)

1. Melt butter in large skillet over medium-high heat. Add onions, mushrooms and salt; cook and stir 20 minutes or until vegetables are browned and most liquid is absorbed. Remove onion mixture to **CROCK-POT**® slow cooker.

2. Stir in stuffing mix and broth. Cover; cook on LOW 3 hours. Garnish with parsley.

BRAISED BEETS WITH CRANBERRIES

MAKES 6 TO 8 SERVINGS

2½ pounds medium beets, peeled and cut into wedges

1 cup cranberry juice

½ cup sweetened dried cranberries

2 tablespoons quick-cooking tapioca

2 tablespoons butter, cubed

2 tablespoons honey

½ teaspoon salt

⅓ cup crumbled blue cheese (optional)

Orange peel, thinly sliced (optional)

1. Combine beets, cranberry juice, cranberries, tapioca, butter, honey and salt in **CROCK-POT**® slow cooker; stir to blend. Cover; cook on LOW 7 to 8 hours.

2. Remove beets to large serving bowl using slotted spoon. Pour half of cooking liquid over beets. Garnish with blue cheese and orange peel.

Five-Ingredient
Mushroom
Stuffing

CANDIED SWEET POTATOES

MAKES 4 SERVINGS

3 medium sweet potatoes (1½ to 2 pounds), sliced into ½-inch rounds

½ cup water

¼ cup (½ stick) butter, cut into small pieces

3 tablespoons sugar

1 tablespoon vanilla

1 teaspoon ground nutmeg

Combine potatoes, water, butter, sugar, vanilla and nutmeg in **CROCK-POT®** slow cooker; stir to blend. Cover; cook on LOW 7 hours or on HIGH 4 hours.

SLOW-COOKED SUCCOTASH

MAKES 8 SERVINGS

2 teaspoons olive oil

1 cup diced onion

1 cup diced green bell pepper

1 cup diced celery

1 teaspoon paprika

1½ cups frozen corn

1½ cups frozen lima beans

1 cup canned diced tomatoes

1 tablespoon minced fresh Italian parsley

Salt and black pepper

1. Heat oil in large skillet over medium heat. Add onion, bell pepper and celery; cook and stir 5 minutes or until vegetables are crisp-tender. Stir in paprika.

2. Stir onion mixture, corn, beans, tomatoes, parsley, salt and black pepper into **CROCK-POT**® slow cooker. Cover; cook on LOW 6 to 8 hours or on HIGH 3 to 4 hours.

GRATIN POTATOES WITH ASIAGO CHEESE

MAKES 4 TO 6 SERVINGS

6 slices bacon, cut into 1-inch pieces

6 medium baking potatoes, peeled and thinly sliced

½ cup grated Asiago cheese

Salt and black pepper

1½ cups whipping cream

1. Heat large skillet over medium heat. Add bacon; cook and stir until crisp. Remove to paper towel-lined plate using slotted spoon.

2. Pour bacon drippings into **CROCK-POT®** slow cooker. Layer one fourth of potatoes on bottom of **CROCK-POT®** slow cooker. Sprinkle one fourth of bacon over potatoes and top with one fourth of cheese. Season with salt and pepper.

3. Repeat layers three times. Pour cream over all. Cover; cook on LOW 7 to 9 hours or on HIGH 5 to 6 hours.

⭐ **TIP:** Fresh potatoes are commercially grown in 48 states in overlapping growing seasons, so at least one or two varieties are always available in the supermarket.

DESSERTS AND DRINKS

TRIPLE CHOCOLATE FANTASY

MAKES 36 PIECES

2 pounds white almond bark, broken into pieces

1 bar (4 ounces) sweetened chocolate, broken into pieces*

1 package (12 ounces) semisweet chocolate chips

2 cups coarsely chopped pecans, toasted**

*Use your favorite high-quality chocolate candy bar.

**To toast pecans, spread in single layer in heavy skillet. Cook and stir over medium heat 1 to 2 minutes or until nuts are lightly browned.

1. Line mini muffin pan with paper baking cups. Place bark, sweetened chocolate and chocolate chips in **CROCK-POT**® slow cooker. Cover; cook on HIGH 1 hour. *Do not stir.*

2. Turn **CROCK-POT**® slow cooker to LOW. Cover; cook on LOW 1 hour, stirring every 15 minutes. Stir in pecans.

3. Drop mixture by tablespoonfuls into prepared baking cups; cool completely. Store in tightly covered container.

STRAWBERRY RHUBARB CRISP

MAKES 8 SERVINGS

FRUIT

- 4 cups sliced hulled fresh strawberries
- 4 cups diced rhubarb (about 5 stalks), cut into ½-inch dice
- 1½ cups granulated sugar
- 2 tablespoons lemon juice
- 1½ tablespoons cornstarch, plus 1 to 2 teaspoons water (optional)

TOPPING

- 1 cup all-purpose flour
- 1 cup old-fashioned oats
- ½ cup granulated sugar
- ½ cup packed brown sugar
- ½ teaspoon ground ginger
- ½ teaspoon ground nutmeg
- ½ cup (1 stick) butter, cubed
- ½ cup sliced almonds, toasted*

To toast almonds, spread in single layer in heavy skillet. Cook and stir over medium heat 1 to 2 minutes or until nuts are lightly browned.

1. Coat inside of **CROCK-POT®** slow cooker with nonstick cooking spray. Combine strawberries, rhubarb, 1½ cups granulated sugar and lemon juice in **CROCK-POT®** slow cooker; stir to blend. Cover; cook on HIGH 1½ hours or until fruit is tender.

2. If fruit is dry after cooking, add a little water. If fruit has too much liquid, mix cornstarch with water; stir into cooking liquid. Cover; cook on HIGH 15 minutes or until thickened.

3. Preheat oven to 375°F. Combine flour, oats, sugars, ginger and nutmeg in medium bowl. Cut in butter using pastry blender or two knives until mixture resembles coarse crumbs. Stir in almonds.

4. Remove lid from **CROCK-POT®** slow cooker and gently sprinkle topping onto fruit. Remove stoneware to oven. Bake 15 to 20 minutes or until topping begins to brown.

TRIPLE DELICIOUS HOT CHOCOLATE

MAKES 6 SERVINGS

3 cups milk, divided

⅓ cup sugar

¼ cup unsweetened cocoa powder

¼ teaspoon salt

¾ teaspoon vanilla

1 cup whipping cream

1 square (1 ounce) bittersweet chocolate, chopped

1 square (1 ounce) white chocolate, chopped

Whipped cream (optional)

Mini semisweet chocolate chips (optional)

1. Combine ½ cup milk, sugar, cocoa and salt in **CROCK-POT®** slow cooker; whisk until smooth. Stir in remaining 2½ cups milk and vanilla. Cover; cook on LOW 2 hours.

2. Stir in cream. Cover; cook on LOW 10 minutes. Stir in bittersweet and white chocolate until melted.

3. Pour hot chocolate into mugs. Top each serving with whipped cream and chocolate chips, if desired.

⭐ **TIP:** Unsweetened cocoa powder is formed by extracting most of the cocoa butter from the nibs of the cocoa bean and grinding the remaining solids into a powder. It is low in fat and contains no additives. It can be stored in a tightly closed container in a cool, dark place for up to two years.

FRUIT AND NUT BAKED APPLES

MAKES 4 SERVINGS

4 large baking apples, such as Rome Beauty or Jonathan

1 tablespoon lemon juice

⅓ cup chopped dried apricots

⅓ cup chopped walnuts or pecans

3 tablespoons packed brown sugar

½ teaspoon ground cinnamon

2 tablespoons unsalted butter, melted

½ cup water

Caramel topping (optional)

1. Scoop out center of each apple, leaving 1½-inch-wide cavity about ½ inch from bottom. Peel top of apple down about 1 inch. Brush peeled edges evenly with lemon juice. Combine apricots, walnuts, brown sugar and cinnamon in small bowl; stir to blend. Add butter; mix well. Spoon mixture evenly into apple cavities.

2. Pour water in bottom of **CROCK-POT**® slow cooker. Place 2 apples in bottom of **CROCK-POT**® slow cooker. Arrange remaining 2 apples above but not directly on top of bottom apples. Cover; cook on LOW 3 to 4 hours or until apples are tender. Serve warm or at room temperature with caramel topping, if desired.

ROCKY ROAD BROWNIE BOTTOMS

MAKES 6 SERVINGS

½ cup packed brown sugar

½ cup water

2 tablespoons unsweetened cocoa powder

2½ cups packaged brownie mix

1 package (about 4 ounces) instant chocolate pudding mix

½ cup milk chocolate chips

2 eggs, beaten

3 tablespoons butter, melted

2 cups mini marshmallows

1 cup chopped pecans or walnuts, toasted*

½ cup chocolate syrup

To toast pecans, spread in single layer in heavy skillet. Cook and stir over medium heat 1 to 2 minutes or until nuts are lightly browned.

1. Prepare foil handles by tearing off three 18×2-inch strips heavy foil (or use regular foil folded to double thickness). Crisscross foil strips in spoke design; place in **CROCK-POT®** slow cooker. Coat inside of **CROCK-POT®** slow cooker with nonstick cooking spray.

2. Combine brown sugar, water and cocoa in small saucepan over medium heat; bring to a boil over medium-high heat. Meanwhile, combine brownie mix, pudding mix, chocolate chips, eggs and butter in medium bowl; stir until well blended. Spread batter in **CROCK-POT®** slow cooker; pour boiling sugar mixture over batter.

3. Cover; cook on HIGH 1½ hours. Turn off heat. Top brownies with marshmallows, pecans and chocolate syrup. Let stand 15 minutes. Use foil handles to lift brownie to large serving platter.

VANILLA SOUR CREAM CHEESECAKE

MAKES 6 TO 8 SERVINGS

¾ cup graham cracker crumbs

¾ cup plus 1 tablespoon sugar, divided

¼ teaspoon ground nutmeg

2 tablespoons unsalted butter, melted

2 packages (8 ounces *each*) cream cheese, softened

3 eggs

½ cup sour cream

1 tablespoon vanilla

3 tablespoons all-purpose flour

Fresh strawberries, sliced (optional)

Sprigs fresh mint (optional)

1. Combine graham cracker crumbs, 1 tablespoon sugar and nutmeg in medium bowl; stir to blend. Stir in butter until well blended. Press mixture into bottom and 1 inch up sides of 6- or 7-inch springform pan.

2. Beat cream cheese in large bowl with electric mixer at high speed 3 to 4 minutes or until smooth. Add remaining ¾ cup sugar; beat 1 to 2 minutes. Beat in eggs, sour cream and vanilla until blended. Stir in flour. Pour batter into crust.

3. Fill 6-quart **CROCK-POT**® slow cooker with ½-inch water and set small wire rack in bottom. Set springform pan on rack. Cover top of stoneware with clean kitchen towel. Cover; cook on HIGH 2 hours.

4. Turn off heat and let stand 1 hour without opening lid. Remove lid; remove cheesecake to wire rack. Cool completely. Cover with plastic wrap; refrigerate 4 to 5 hours or until well chilled.

5. To serve, run tip of knife around edge of cheesecake and remove springform mold. Top with strawberries, if desired. Garnish with mint. Cut into wedges to serve.

GINGER PEAR CIDER

MAKES 8 TO 10 SERVINGS

8 cups pear juice or cider

¾ cup lemon juice

¼ to ½ cup honey

10 whole cloves

2 whole cinnamon sticks, plus additional for garnish

8 slices fresh ginger

1. Combine pear juice, lemon juice, honey, cloves, 2 cinnamon sticks and ginger in 5-quart **CROCK-POT**® slow cooker.

2. Cover; cook on LOW 5 to 6 hours or on HIGH 2½ to 3 hours. Remove and discard cloves, cinnamon sticks and ginger before serving. Garnish with additional cinnamon sticks.

WARM HONEY LEMONADE

MAKES 9 CUPS

4½ cups water
2½ cups lemon juice
1 cup orange juice

1 cup honey
¼ cup sugar
Lemon slices (optional)

1. Combine water, lemon juice, orange juice, honey and sugar in **CROCK-POT®** slow cooker; whisk well.

2. Cover; cook on LOW 2 hours. Whisk well before serving. Garnish with lemon slices.

MIXED BERRY COBBLER

MAKES 8 SERVINGS

1 package (16 ounces) frozen mixed berries

½ cup granulated sugar

2 tablespoons quick-cooking tapioca

2 teaspoons grated lemon peel

1½ cups all-purpose flour

½ cup packed light brown sugar

2¼ teaspoons baking powder

¼ teaspoon ground nutmeg

½ cup milk

⅓ cup butter, melted

Vanilla ice cream (optional)

1. Coat inside of **CROCK-POT**® slow cooker with nonstick cooking spray. Combine berries, granulated sugar, tapioca and lemon peel in **CROCK-POT**® slow cooker; stir to blend.

2. Combine flour, brown sugar, baking powder and nutmeg in medium bowl. Add milk and butter; stir just until blended. Drop spoonfuls of dough on top of berry mixture. Cover; cook on LOW 4 hours. Turn off heat. Uncover; let stand 30 minutes. Serve with ice cream, if desired.

⭐ **TIP:** Cobblers are popular American fruit-based desserts. They are similar to deep-dish pies, but have a rich, thick biscuit topping. The biscuit topping should not be smoothed out but left bumpy and rough, or "cobbled." Cobblers can also be served with whipped cream instead of ice cream.

LUSCIOUS PECAN BREAD PUDDING

MAKES 6 SERVINGS

3 cups day-old French bread cubes

3 tablespoons chopped pecans, toasted*

2¼ cups milk

2 eggs, beaten

½ cup sugar

1 teaspoon vanilla

¾ teaspoon ground cinnamon, divided

¾ cup cranberry juice cocktail

1½ cups frozen pitted tart cherries

2 tablespoons sugar

*To toast pecans, spread in single layer in heavy skillet. Cook and stir over medium heat 1 to 2 minutes or until nuts are lightly browned.

1. Prepare foil handles by tearing off three 18×2-inch strips heavy foil (or use regular foil folded to double thickness). Crisscross foil strips in spoke design; place in **CROCK-POT**® slow cooker. Toss bread cubes and pecans in soufflé dish that fits inside of **CROCK-POT**® slow cooker.

2. Combine milk, eggs, sugar, vanilla and ½ teaspoon cinnamon in large bowl; pour over bread mixture in soufflé dish. Cover tightly with foil. Place soufflé dish in **CROCK-POT**® slow cooker. Pour hot water into **CROCK-POT**® slow cooker to about 1½ inches from top of soufflé dish. Cover; cook on LOW 2 to 3 hours.

3. Meanwhile, combine cranberry juice and remaining ¼ teaspoon cinnamon in small saucepan; stir in cherries. Bring to a boil over medium heat; cook 5 minutes. Remove from heat. Stir in sugar.

4. Lift soufflé dish from **CROCK-POT**® slow cooker using foil handles. Serve bread pudding with cherry sauce.

CHERRY DELIGHT

MAKES 8 TO 10 SERVINGS

1 can (21 ounces) cherry pie
filling

1 package (about 18 ounces)
yellow cake mix

½ cup (1 stick) butter, melted

⅓ cup chopped walnuts

Coat inside of **CROCK-POT**® slow cooker with nonstick cooking spray. Place pie filling in **CROCK-POT**® slow cooker. Combine cake mix and butter in medium bowl. Spread evenly over pie filling. Sprinkle with walnuts. Cover; cook on LOW 3 to 4 hours or on HIGH 1½ to 2 hours.

SPICED VANILLA APPLESAUCE

MAKES 6 CUPS

5 pounds (about 10 medium) sweet apples (such as Fuji or Gala), peeled and cut into 1-inch pieces

½ cup water

2 teaspoons vanilla

1 teaspoon ground cinnamon

¼ teaspoon ground nutmeg

¼ teaspoon ground cloves

1. Combine apples, water, vanilla, cinnamon, nutmeg and cloves in **CROCK-POT®** slow cooker; stir to blend. Cover; cook on HIGH 3 to 4 hours or until apples are very tender.

2. Turn off heat. Mash mixture with potato masher to smooth out any large lumps. Let cool completely before serving.

FUDGE AND CREAM PUDDING CAKE

MAKES 8 TO 10 SERVINGS

2 tablespoons unsalted butter

1 cup all-purpose flour

½ cup packed light brown sugar

5 tablespoons unsweetened cocoa powder, divided

2 teaspoons baking powder

½ teaspoon ground cinnamon

⅛ teaspoon salt

1 cup whipping cream

1 tablespoon vegetable oil

1 teaspoon vanilla

1½ cups hot water

½ cup packed dark brown sugar

Whipped cream (optional)

1. Prepare foil handles by tearing off three 18×2-inch strips heavy foil (or use regular foil folded to double thickness). Crisscross foil strips in spoke design; place in **CROCK-POT**® slow cooker. Coat inside of 5-quart **CROCK-POT**® slow cooker and foil handles with nonstick cooking spray.

2. Combine flour, light brown sugar, 3 tablespoons cocoa, baking powder, cinnamon and salt in medium bowl. Add whipping cream, oil and vanilla; stir to blend. Pour batter into **CROCK-POT**® slow cooker.

3. Combine hot water, dark brown sugar and remaining 2 tablespoons cocoa in medium bowl; stir to blend. Pour sauce over cake batter. *Do not stir.* Cover; cook on HIGH 2 hours. Turn off heat. Let stand 10 minutes.

4. Remove to large plate using foil handles. Discard foil. Cut into wedges to serve and serve with whipped cream, if desired.

BANANAS FOSTER

MAKES 12 SERVINGS

12 bananas, cut into quarters
1 cup flaked coconut
1 cup dark corn syrup
⅔ cup butter, melted
¼ cup lemon juice
2 teaspoons grated lemon peel

2 teaspoons rum
1 teaspoon ground cinnamon
½ teaspoon salt
12 slices prepared pound cake
1 quart vanilla ice cream

1. Combine bananas and coconut in **CROCK-POT®** slow cooker. Combine corn syrup, butter, lemon juice, lemon peel, rum, cinnamon and salt in medium bowl; stir to blend. Pour over bananas.

2. Cover; cook on LOW 1 to 2 hours. To serve, arrange bananas on pound cake slices. Top with ice cream and warm sauce.

WARM PEANUT-CARAMEL DIP

MAKES 1¾ CUPS

¾ cup peanut butter
¾ cup caramel topping

⅓ cup milk
1 apple, thinly sliced

1. Combine peanut butter, caramel topping and milk in medium saucepan; cook over medium heat until smooth and creamy, stirring occasionally.

2. Coat inside of **CROCK-POT®** "No-Dial" slow cooker with nonstick cooking spray. Fill with warm dip. Serve with apples.

Bananas
Foster

S'MORES FONDUE

MAKES ABOUT 4 CUPS

1 pound milk chocolate, chopped

2 jars (7 ounces *each*) marshmallow creme

⅔ cup half-and-half

2 teaspoons vanilla

1 cup mini marshmallows

Banana slices, apple slices, fresh strawberries and graham crackers

1. Combine chocolate, marshmallow creme, half-and-half and vanilla in **CROCK-POT**® slow cooker. Cover; cook on LOW 1½ to 3 hours, stirring after 1 hour.

2. Sprinkle top of fondue with mini marshmallows. Serve with banana and apple slices, strawberries and graham crackers.

WARM SPICED APPLES AND PEARS

MAKES 6 SERVINGS

½ cup (1 stick) butter

1 vanilla bean

1 cup packed brown sugar

½ cup water

½ lemon, sliced

1 whole cinnamon stick, broken in half

½ teaspoon ground cloves

5 pears, cored and quartered

5 small Granny Smith apples, cored and quartered

1. Melt butter in medium saucepan over medium heat. Cut vanilla bean in half and scrape out seeds. Add seeds and pod, brown sugar, water, lemon slices, cinnamon stick halves and cloves to saucepan. Bring to a boil; cook 1 minute, stirring constantly. Remove from heat.

2. Combine pears, apples and butter mixture in **CROCK-POT**® slow cooker; stir to blend. Cover; cook on LOW 3½ to 4 hours or on HIGH 2 hours, stirring every 45 minutes. Remove vanilla pod and cinnamon stick halves before serving.

S'mores Fondue

SPICED APPLE TEA

MAKES 4 SERVINGS

3 bags cinnamon herbal tea

3 cups boiling water

2 cups unsweetened apple juice

6 whole cloves

1 whole cinnamon stick

1. Place tea bags in **CROCK-POT®** slow cooker. Pour boiling water over tea bags; cover and let steep 10 minutes. Remove and discard tea bags.

2. Add apple juice, cloves and cinnamon stick to **CROCK-POT®** slow cooker. Cover; cook on LOW 2 to 3 hours. Remove and discard cloves and cinnamon stick. Serve warm in mugs.

HOT TODDIES

MAKES 10 SERVINGS

8 cups water

2 cups bourbon

¾ cup honey

⅔ cup lemon juice

1 (1-inch) piece ginger, peeled and cut into 4 slices

1 whole cinnamon stick

Lemon slices (optional)

1. Combine water, bourbon, honey, lemon juice, ginger and cinnamon stick in **CROCK-POT**® slow cooker; stir to blend. Cover; cook on HIGH 2 hours. Turn **CROCK-POT**® slow cooker to WARM.

2. Remove and discard cinnamon stick and ginger pieces. Ladle into individual mugs; garnish with lemon slices.

POACHED AUTUMN FRUITS WITH VANILLA-CITRUS BROTH

MAKES 6 SERVINGS

2 Granny Smith apples, peeled, cored and halved (reserve cores)

2 Bartlett pears, peeled, cored and halved (reserve cores)

1 orange, peeled and halved

⅓ cup sugar

¼ cup plus 1 tablespoon honey

1 vanilla bean, split and seeded (reserve seeds)

1 whole cinnamon stick

Dried cranberries (optional)

Vanilla ice cream (optional)

1. Place apple and pear cores in **CROCK-POT**® slow cooker. Squeeze juice from orange halves into **CROCK-POT**® slow cooker. Add orange halves, sugar, honey, vanilla bean and seeds and cinnamon stick. Add apples, pears and enough water to cover fruit; stir to combine. Cover; cook on HIGH 2 hours or until fruit is tender.

2. Remove apple and pear halves; dice. Strain cooking liquid; discard solids. Return fruit and liquid to **CROCK-POT**® slow cooker. Stir in cranberries, if desired. Cover; cook on HIGH 10 to 15 minutes or until thickened. To serve, spoon fruit with sauce evenly into bowls. Top with vanilla ice cream, if desired.

METRIC CONVERSION CHART

VOLUME MEASUREMENTS (dry)

$1/8$ teaspoon = 0.5 mL
$1/4$ teaspoon = 1 mL
$1/2$ teaspoon = 2 mL
$3/4$ teaspoon = 4 mL
1 teaspoon = 5 mL
1 tablespoon = 15 mL
2 tablespoons = 30 mL
$1/4$ cup = 60 mL
$1/3$ cup = 75 mL
$1/2$ cup = 125 mL
$2/3$ cup = 150 mL
$3/4$ cup = 175 mL
1 cup = 250 mL
2 cups = 1 pint = 500 mL
3 cups = 750 mL
4 cups = 1 quart = 1 L

VOLUME MEASUREMENTS (fluid)

1 fluid ounce (2 tablespoons) = 30 mL
4 fluid ounces ($1/2$ cup) = 125 mL
8 fluid ounces (1 cup) = 250 mL
12 fluid ounces ($1 1/2$ cups) = 375 mL
16 fluid ounces (2 cups) = 500 mL

WEIGHTS (mass)

$1/2$ ounce = 15 g
1 ounce = 30 g
3 ounces = 90 g
4 ounces = 120 g
8 ounces = 225 g
10 ounces = 285 g
12 ounces = 360 g
16 ounces = 1 pound = 450 g

DIMENSIONS

$1/16$ inch = 2 mm
$1/8$ inch = 3 mm
$1/4$ inch = 6 mm
$1/2$ inch = 1.5 cm
$3/4$ inch = 2 cm
1 inch = 2.5 cm

OVEN TEMPERATURES

250°F = 120°C
275°F = 140°C
300°F = 150°C
325°F = 160°C
350°F = 180°C
375°F = 190°C
400°F = 200°C
425°F = 220°C
450°F = 230°C

BAKING PAN SIZES

Utensil	Size in Inches/Quarts	Metric Volume	Size in Centimeters
Baking or Cake Pan (square or rectangular)	8×8×2	2 L	20×20×5
	9×9×2	2.5 L	23×23×5
	12×8×2	3 L	30×20×5
	13×9×2	3.5 L	33×23×5
Loaf Pan	8×4×3	1.5 L	20×10×7
	9×5×3	2 L	23×13×7
Round Layer Cake Pan	8×1½	1.2 L	20×4
	9×1½	1.5 L	23×4
Pie Plate	8×1¼	750 mL	20×3
	9×1¼	1 L	23×3
Baking Dish or Casserole	1 quart	1 L	—
	1½ quart	1.5 L	—
	2 quart	2 L	—